About the Author

Jim was born in the dockside town of Birkenhead Merseyside. At 18, he joined the Royal Navy. Upon leaving he travelled and worked in Europe, America, Canada and Australia. Finally, the author retrained as a landscape gardener, highlighted by managing landscaping of Adventure Land Disney Land Paris.

Jim met Cherry in 1984 and bought his first husky, Hustler, in 1987. This changed his life and began his lifetime passion for dogsledding. The author retired to France in 2012 where he lives with Cherry, his 6 remaining huskies, 4 cats and Wizzy, the Border Terrier.

For the dogs that started me on my way:
Hustler, Cassie, Labbi and Gabbi.

For the Zeros that changed my life:
Maji, Bandit, Cougar, Raider, Dansa and Fly.
Especially for my chien de tête extraordinaire
JOKER.

And for the dogs still with me, showing the way:
Angel, her pups Bear, Reef and Django.

And of course,
my Chef de meute,

Gun

To Cherry Burton – without whom none of this would have been possible.

Jim Bryde

SLED DOG GUN:
AVIEMORE DREAMING

Copyright © Jim Bryde (2015)

The right of Jim Bryde to be identified as author of this work has been asserted by him in accordance with section 77 and 78 of the Copyright, Designs and Patents Act 1988.

All rights reserved. No part of this publication may be reproduced, stored in a retrieval system, or transmitted in any form or by any means, electronic, mechanical, photocopying, recording, or otherwise, without the prior permission of the publishers.

Any person who commits any unauthorized act in relation to this publication may be liable to criminal prosecution and civil claims for damages.

A CIP catalogue record for this title is available from the British Library.

Cover photo taken by Don James.

ISBN 978 1 78455 227 5 (Paperback)
ISBN 978 1 78455 229 9 (Hardback)

www.austinmacauley.com

First Published (2015)
Austin Macauley Publishers Ltd.
25 Canada Square
Canary Wharf
London
E14 5LB

Printed and bound in Great Britain

Acknowledgments

My sister Norma and partner 'Paddy' Bernie, their daughters, Kate and Jessica and my nephew Matthew, for all the help in the early years looking after the dogs.

The Finnegan Family – Hughie, Miriam and two grandkids, Luke and Carl, for all the help, assistance and cups of tea over the past 25 years.

The Keen Family – Paul, Amanda and daughter Katie for looking after Gun when I was unable to take him France when I first retired.

Harris Dunlop – for breeding the wonderful Zero dogs.

Steve Radburn – for having the knowledge and guts to bring the Zeros to Britain.

Don James – for the wonderful cover photo of Gun.

Gareth Bowyer – for making an 'old man' delirious for taking on 7 lunatic pups and training them to be Britain's best ever team.

Fred Allen and Kirk Matthews, for giving me my winning Lottery tickets, Fly and Angel respectively.

Penny Evans, for her wonderful foreword and finally believing I could write!!!

Bru and Jenny for Cassie and Hustler.

Steve, Vicki, Charlie and Jo, for helping me out by taking in and looking after Bear, Gun, Angel and Reef in my time of need.

Lord March – in providing me with the best training ground I would ever need – Selhurst Park, Goodwood Estate.

To all members of the best club in the World – S.H.C.G.B. for providing me with the venue to fulfil my dreams – Aviemore.

To Bob, Paul, Mike, Roger, and Carol for providing, unwittingly, chapter titles.

And finally, Joker – my dog in a million.

Contents

Foreword	15
Chapter 1	17
It's Just Another Day December 22nd 2002	
Chapter 2	22
Aviemore, The Dream Starts	
Chapter 3	30
50 Shades of Yellow	
Chapter 4	39
Gun: A Year in the Life	
Chapter 5	43
Training Begins	
Chapter 6	55
Coming of Age	
Chapter 7	62
The Dogs and Equipment	
Chapter 8	66
Equipment and Rules	
Chapter 9	68
Aviemore 2004 The Race: B class	
Chapter 10	73
Reflections	
Chapter 11	76
Fame at Last... I Think Not	
Chapter 12	84
Decisions	
Photos	91
Chapter 13	121
Aviemore 2005 $22^{nd} - 23^{rd}$ January	
Chapter14	134
Mixed Emotions	
Chapter 15	144
Winds of Change	
Chapter 16	152
I Hear You Knocking	

Chapter 17 156
Angel
Chapter 18 160
You're Moving Out Today!
Chapter 19 163
Lost in France
Chapter 20 170
Aviemore 2009 Between Blue and Me
Chapter 21 175
The Trio Return
Chapter 22 188
Run Like the Wind
Chapter 23 192
Jokerman
Chapter 24 194
Shadow on the Wall
Chapter 25 200
In My Own Time
Chapter 26 206
Aviemore 2011 Three Wheels on my Wagon
Chapter 27 218
It's Just Another Day Sunday Morning January 26, 2014, France

Foreword

I was surprised when Jim contacted me and said he'd written a book. Surely not the Clown Prince of UK sled dog races ... You'd think after all these years I wouldn't fall into the usual trap of ... "Joker Jim done what?" but to my discredit that's what I did. Every walk of life has its mavericks – someone who doesn't always completely follow the rules but makes life just that bit more colourful in the process – and Jim is our UK sled dog racing renegade. But woe betide those who take him for a fool. Like his dogs Jim lives life at full tilt which may be unsettling for some but his insight and understanding of sled dogs and their training and racing is remarkable, even though his show career never truly took off with the same success. Yes, I was the judge he chose to enter Gun under. A fourth was the best I could give to a dog who could not manage four feet on the ground at the same time, but with a bit more effort he would easily have qualified for Crufts – you don't win races with dogs that have poor construction. But racing is Jim's home ground and his training regimes caused the UK Mushers to sit up and take life a bit more seriously ... oh and remember to take hangover cures to races!

In this book Jim opens a very honest and frank door on his life with his dogs. Read and learn from this generous guy who so clearly loves his dogs but who – like so many of us – in his love affair with this eccentric and most beautiful breed, the Siberian Husky, has been forced to understand they live life to their rules not always ours. Admire his efforts, laugh at his antics and cry as we all have to when the time comes for our cherished four-footed friends to leave us.

I hope those lucky French racers are enjoying his company because UK Sled Dog Races are just that bit lacking now he has crossed The Channel.

Penny Evans
Secretary of the Siberian Husky Club of GB 1978-2005
Co-organiser of the SHCGB Aviemore Sled Dog Race 1984-2006
KC and FCI CC qualified Judge of Siberian Huskies
Breeder of Siberian Huskies 1977-200 under Mikalya and 2000 to present under Penkhala affixes

Chapter 1

It's Just Another Day

December 22nd 2002

Gun at 3 weeks old

And yet it all started so well.

Cherry and I had been out the night before for a meal, so I was up a bit later than usual, but not too late to take the dogs out for their Sunday run.

We were in training for an 8 stage race, the 9th running of "The Trophie de Savoie" (which was starting on 4th January) and I was so glad that the incessant rain of the past two weeks had at least stopped for a couple of hours. The weather was now cold and dry and I was looking forward to hooking up my seven dogs, Joker, Dansa, DiMaggio (Magi), Bandit, Cougar, Raider, and my only girl, Fly. All pure bred Siberian Huskies, the original sled dogs.

I had been running them hard now for the past month, 5 miles a day, four times a week, over the hilly terrain of Selhurst Park, Goodwood to get them at least some way prepared for the coming adventures in the French Alps – though I have to admit Selhurst Park in December really doesn't bear much resemblance to Meribel, (the venue for the first stage), but it helps to dream.

All the dogs where motoring along the trail, including Fly in lead, even though she did look a bit fatter than usual, but I put that down to the fact I'd been feeding them all more to get their body weight up a bit in preparation for the minus 20c temperatures they would be experiencing in the two weeks in France.

So after a very fast run, I loaded the dogs and quad back into the truck and drove the 6 miles to my house at Runcton (south of Chichester). There it was a quick unload, feed and water and then into the house for something I'd been looking forward to for weeks, the Liverpool –Everton derby match on the tele.

Wasn't much of a game, usual frenzied action accompanied by the flurry of fouls, but no goals by half-time. So got up, as you do, to put the kettle on for the regulation cup of tea, when I heard the dulcet tones of Cherry, my partner of 19 years, ring out; "There's a big racket going on out in the pens, I'm trying to work here, go and get it sorted", or words to that effect.

"Those bloody dogs, 5 miles and they still won't settle down!" I was heard to mutter as I went out to the dog pen. No matter how hard you ran them and how knackered they appeared to be at the finish, by the time you got them home, they were full of beans and raring to go again. Not that I was totally surprised, these dogs where bred to run 60/70 miles a day pulling a loaded sled, so 5 miles was a stroll in the park to them. But this was sunny England not the frozen wastes of Siberia, no matter what they thought, and 5 miles was ample. They were going to settle down whether they liked it or not!

Anyway popped my head into the offending pen, expecting to find the usual suspects Magi and Bandit arguing over whose turn it was to sleep in the box nearest to the door. There were ample sleeping boxes in the compound, 5 for the 4 dogs but these two still argued over where to sleep. Wouldn't mind but it was a different box each day. Just bloody minded those two.

To my surprise though, the three males Magi, Bandit, and Raider, were all sitting upright looking over towards the furthest box with, I swear, a look of astonishment on their faces, or was I imagining it?

But where was Fly?

If she's escaped (Siberians are excellent escape artistes), I would have a very long afternoon trying to find her, us living in a very rural position, which was like a kiddies' playground to a sibe on the loose. DiMaggio had once escaped and came back to the house (yes they will return of their own free will... eventually.) but with a very badly damaged mouth, which a trip to the vets the next day left him minus 6 teeth. On his escapade he'd tangled with a herd of Highland cattle and came off worse.

Calling her – nothing, not a murmur, except the three males jumping all over me.

Nothing for it but to phone the relevant authorities, and then get the boots on and go and look for her. Trouble was I still couldn't see how she could have escaped, and then... movement in the furthest box.

Fly, at this stage, was not very good at answering to her name, so I should not have been too surprised that she had failed to answer yet again. I had only had her for 6 months as she had been returned to her breeder because her new owner didn't want her anymore (couldn't control her was the real reason) and now 2 years old she was not yet fully integrated into my pack, and still needed more training on the socialising side. But, and it was a big but, she was a very good sled dog with a very good pedigree, her father was my own lead dog Joker, so she had, in a sense, come home.

Cursing and calling her all the names under the sun, I looked in the box to see our Fly all curled up and wagging her tail. Wagging her tail! I don't believe this dog wagging her tail, she should be out jumping all over me like all the others.

Then I noticed she was licking something. So that's it she's dug up a bone, won't let anyone take it from her and is guarding it with her life.

And then it moved!

Double take here, moving bone?

Must have caught something that had crawled into the pen, bird, hedgehog, snake (No, too cold for a snake)

Better have a decent look just in case, and then the shock of my life.

She was licking a brown and white new-born puppy!

Now I may not be the sharpest tool in the box, but my mind was going 10 to the dozen... HOW?!

Pulled myself together a bit and did what any sane person would do, panic and call Cherry.

She came out, rightly annoyed as I had been sent out specifically to deal with this situation, and in her agitated state had now obviously decided I had failed and she was going to fix it.

She assessed the whole situation in a glance and came out with (Rather too smugly if you ask me) "I told you she was pregnant you divvy". Bit strong that, especially coming out with a slang word from my Merseyside home, Birkenhead.

But then I remembered the accidental mating that had taken place in September whilst I was out house hunting in Spain. I remembered it clearly, the phone call still ringing in my ears as I answered it to be told "Your bloody dog Magi has mated that bloody Fly, and the noise she made has woken up half of West Sussex" Oops! (If you've ever heard the racket dogs can make when being mated you'll understand)

Now you might think, quite rightly, that I should have noticed that Fly was pregnant, but Siberians are not your usual dog. She had not missed a beat in training, had been seen by a vet's assistant 1 month earlier "no she's not pregnant, can't feel a thing" (famous last words), and only the previous week, had run on a 6 dog team in a Siberian Husky Club rally at Trentham Gardens (Stoke) in front of the whole club and nobody had said a word. And why would they, to look at her she was still a long lean running machine.

So feeling a bit of a fool, ok a big fool, I picked up mother and newly born daughter, brought them into the house, made a makeshift bed for them in the kitchen, kicked the cat out, made that cup of tea and settled down to watch the rest of the match, uninterrupted or so I hoped.

Ten minutes later, thump, and out pops puppy no 2, a large brown male.

Well that's it then, she can't have any more in there, she's not big enough, so after checking all was fine, went back to watch the match... again.

That finished 0-0 which was a huge disappointment to me (a lifelong 'Kopite')

But what happened next wasn't.

One more "thud", another trip to the kitchen and there on the blanket was a jet black, big boned Siberian husky puppy.

That date 22nd December 2002 was to have a profound effect on me that would culminate just over 8 years later on 23rd January 2011 at Aviemore, Scotland.

This is the story of those 8 years and a dog called Gun.

Chapter 2

Aviemore, The Dream Starts

"To be the best, you've got to beat the rest. That's all there is to it" Adam Vinatieri

And to do that in husky racing in Britain, that means winning, and winning at the home of racing, Aviemore.

Nothing else counts.

Aviemore. Say that to a "musher" in Britain and stand back and be prepared for a long narrative. To the musher it means only one thing, Sled dog racing at its finest.

Aviemore is situated just south of Inverness on the A9, in the heart of the Scottish Highlands. It forms part of the Cairngorms, and is perhaps famous for being the premier ski-resort in Britain.

But it is also famous for an activity that is more associated with the frozen wilds of Alaska, Dog Sledding.

Every January, (usually the 3rd weekend), sees the arrival of some 200 "mushers" and their dogs for the annual sled dog race organised by The Siberian Husky Club Of great Britain.

This event has been run since 1984, (when 12 hardy teams competed in the inaugural race,) to what is now arguably the biggest sled dog race in the World, in terms of entrants at least.

Now lots of people have heard of the race in Alaska, The Iditarod, even if they can't quite recall its name. It is often referred to as "The Last Great Race on Earth", and I personally think you need to be nuts to enter it. It's run through the wastes of Alaska, starting from downtown Anchorage to the finish on Main Street Nome, a distance of 1100 miles in temperatures that can go down to minus 70c, on the back of a sled pulled by 18 highly trained dogs, travelling on average 120 miles a day. The winner nowadays finishes round about the 9 day mark, totally exhausted, but beaming with pride. To even finish is an achievement, but to win, legends are made of this.

Contrast that with our "Iditarod" – 4 miles (Saturday and Sunday) racing for all competitors save juniors and 8 dog entrants, a combined time of 26 minutes for the two days for the course record, and it's no wonder that most members of the public have no idea that dog sledding actually takes place in Britain. "Can't be that exciting! Never seen it on the television, and your dogs look too small, you sure they are Huskies?" Are some of the usual responses when I tell people my hobby and show them the dogs. But you'd be wrong. And if you watch closely, from November to the end of March, you'll see dedicated souls driving various forms of transport up and down the motorways of Britain, trying to get to the race meetings that have been organised, so they can participate with their dogs in this most Arctic of sports.

I've been part of this dubious parade ever since I entered a teach–in for Rookie dog runners held in mid Wales in 1989.

Here in Britain, due to the lack of snow, if you want to race dogs, you have to come up with a different method other than sleds for the very simple reason, they don't work on gravel/grass trails.

So the original "dirty dozen" mushers at Aviemore competed on the trails driving, what can only be described as, tanks on wheels. These contraptions were extremely heavy and cumbersome, and utilised the wheels borrowed from Vespas/Lambrettas, the Mods of the days' favourite transport. Speed was pedestrian to say the least, and having ridden one once myself, I'm amazed no one was seriously injured racing them on the very fast down-hills that Aviemore is famous and notorious for.

How times have changed.

Nowadays, my own "rig" weighs in around 15kgs, is made of aluminium tubing, has hydraulic rear disc brakes, carbon fibre handlebars and wheels and tyres that resemble those that adorn "The Tour de France" bikes. Eat your heart out Mark Cavendish.

The dogs also have undergone a similar transformation.

My first dog which I bought in 1987, was what most people would imagine a Siberian Husky to look like. Big boned, heavy, grey/white (but no blue eyes!) and a thick double coat. He looked the part, you could imagine him pulling a sled all day and not being tired at the end. But he was slow. The first race I ever won was with him leading at an average speed of 12 mph. And I won, so what speed were the rest doing?

Contrast that with my current team, of Zero line dogs.

All of them long and lean, with much shorter coats, and capable of running and winning at a 20mph average.

Couple that with the very light rig, and the sport of dog sledding has evolved into an extreme test of nerve and courage.

In France, where I now live, they have banned these racing rigs calling them "tres dangereux" and look at me as though I am a complete "imbecile" (With the added gesture of finger pointed to the head, a universal language that needs no explanation) when I tell them we run up to 8 dogs with them in Britain.

But this is what we use in Britain, and we tend to be very good at it.

And Aviemore is the pinnacle of the sport in Britain.

Win that and you are the best, no questions asked.

Sure, like every other sport, there are organisations who try to claim to have the best, and Dog sledding in Britain is no exception.

In Britain in the early 90's, all races were organised by the Siberian Husky Club of GB. But 2 events around that time had a profound effect on the sport which still exists to this day.

The first event was unwittingly started by a guy called Steve Radburn who had the guts and knowledge to challenge the order of the day and import dogs from the World Championship kennels of New York racer Harris Dunlap. These dogs had taken America and Europe by storm and carried the Kennel club breeders' name "Zero". Steve also imported another dog of proven Swedish lines; "Rookies Woody" and when he formed his own kennels by mating these dogs, they consequently started to win the races they entered, obliterating the established stars of the day. Ultimately, this proved his undoing and he was hounded (no pun intended) out of the sport a few years later, with muttered accusations of his dogs not being purebred, but crossed with the Alaskan Husky (a much faster dog) ringing in his ears.

The second was a race series organised by Labatts who had a big promotional drive going at the time featuring Siberian Huskies. For the series, entrants had their mileage paid to and from the races from their home address to the tune of 12p per mile. This in 1993/94 was a fortune to impoverished mushers and consequently the races were very well attended.

Unfortunately, a couple of girl mushers started to beat the "stars of the day" thus upsetting the apple cart and threatening to destroy the status quo. The fact that these two girls were amongst the first two people to get their hands on these "Zero" dogs did not go unnoticed.

Because a precedent had already been set by having a series of races organised by people other than the SHCGB, these "stars" saw their chance. They formed their own race organisation "BSDRA" and put their own race calendar together. Nothing in the rules to say they couldn't do this, it's a free democratic country we live in, and theoretically anyone with access to a few Forest trails could do the same. And they did. More races for everyone can only be a good thing you'd think. More choice of venue. So instead of having to travel the length of Britain, there was a good chance that another organisation would have a venue near you. Great news and we all looked forward to the following year's racing calendar being published.

And then the bombshell.

"Any dogs with Zero lines in the 5 generation pedigree will not be allowed to enter the BSRDA series"

For clarification all pedigree dogs in Britain are registered at The Kennel Club of GB. You can trace the pedigree of your own dog by purchasing a 5 pedigree chart, showing your dog's grandparents, great grandparents, etc. As you have to give your dog's kennel club name and parent's names on the entry form for races, BSDRA had you by the proverbial "short and curlies".

This caused outrage within the husky circuit, threats and counter threats bouncing around like ping pong balls. It was not unusual to go to dog races to see miffed mushers wearing T-shirts/Sweatshirts with various slogans on them, but all bearing the same basic message "Zeros, if you can't beat them, ban them!"

Eventually the main organisers of BSDRA (who were then, and are still now, members of the SHCGB) were summoned to an extraordinary club meeting to explain themselves, and why they were banning club members from racing their kennel club registered dogs at BSDRA rallies.

Two answers were forthcoming.

1- Zero dogs were dominating the scene in Europe and BSDRA wanted to try and keep the original breeds pure in Britain and maintain the old lines.

2- Zero dogs were about 2 miles per hour faster than the dogs currently in Britain, and they didn't want them dominating like they do in Europe!

In effect "it's my ball and if you don't let me win you can't play!" So you now have an organisation in Britain which proudly boasts that it organises some of the finest races in the country, has its own "champion racers" but bans the teams that have Zero dogs because they will win. It's a bit like American baseball having a world series, but only American teams can enter. A complete and utter nonsense!

Far-fetched?

Not really, that rule is still in operation today and a quick glance at the now renamed BSHRA web site says "All purebred sled-dogs can enter "but excluding those dogs with Zero Bloodlines". Racial segregation in a Free Country like Britain lives!

You couldn't make it up if you tried.

But returning to real racing and Aviemore.

Races here are held over 2 days. Saturday and Sunday with the initial order of starting being drawn out of the hat on the Friday evening Mushers meeting. The main races are 8 dog racing over 7 miles and then 6/4/3/2 dogs held over 4 miles. You go off at 2 minute intervals (like time trialling in bike racing) for the 8 and 6 dog, with 1 minute intervals for the 4/3/2 dogs. And this is where Aviemore gets its claim to be the biggest race venue in the world. The Iditarod maybe attracts 80 entrants, Yukon Quest 50, and most other races between 60-140 entrants. I've raced at Aviemore against over 50 entrants in a 4 dog class alone!

When you bring your dogs to race here they have got to be very fit and very well trained, and you yourself have to have nerves of steel to get the best out of them, especially in the two races that require the least help from the musher (driver); 4 dog and 6 dog.

In the 8 dog the fact that you have to do the circuit twice, mushing up a very steep hill on the 2nd circuit means you get off and run. If you don't you won't win, and most probably won't get home till it's dark and everyone else has gone home; simple as that.

In 2 and 3 dog the fitness of the musher is paramount for winning, unless of course you are a female weighing in at around 6/7 stone. I'll explain.

Dog sled-racing is, I believe, unique in the sporting world. There is no age or gender barrier. Once you are 16 you can turn up at the start line with your dogs and race. No concessions are given. It is not uncommon to see a 70 year old male musher followed out of the starting chute by a 16 year old girl. All the rules are centred on the dogs and equipment.

At Aviemore, the start of the race is along a very fast twisting but FLAT course for the first 300mts, and then a right turn brings you to a hill, a very long steep uphill. You can win and lose the race in the next few minutes depending on numerous factors here. If you are either fat or unfit, (or both) the next 3/4 minutes will be hell. Two dogs cannot pull a heavyweight up that hill, you have to get off and run. So if you are a bloke of about 14 stone average weight, I hope you have prepared for this. Because flying by you up the hill being pulled up it, will be the lightweight 6/7 stone girl, your competitor. Bye, Bye as you see her backside disappearing up the trail as you are puffing and blowing trying to get to the crest. You'll struggle to catch her on the very fast 2 mile section that is all downhill, where turning right to run alongside the slight uphill alongside the Loch, you might make up a bit of time on her, before the killer of a hill about 800mts from the finish, you will see her disappear again, as you crest the hill and watch her in the distance cross the finish line ahead of you. But times and attitudes are changing, so you will now see fit looking Lycra clad blokes lining up at the start and doing as much running as the dogs. It does dismay me to see Mushers cross the finish line in front, yes, IN FRONT of their dogs, and practically collapse frothing at the mouth once there. Come on fellas it's called "dog sledding"; the dogs pull you not the other way around!

Contrast that with a highly trained fit 4/6 dog team. Try and get off and run with that lot is verging on either being very stupid or suicidal. The dogs are pulling the rig and feeling resistance, **you**, all the time you run. By keeping the tug line tight, you make sure that all that power is transferred into pulling you along at the fastest speed possible. You get off, the dogs suddenly have a lighter load to pull, and immediately speed up, alarmingly so, with the obvious consequences. The musher either fails to get back on the rig in time, misses his step and either lets go and has a long walk home to find a completely destroyed rig, or trips, hangs on for dear life and finishes the race with completely destroyed knees. Racing dogs rarely, if ever, understand stop, no matter how frantic you scream it. Take your pick!

So there you are, on the start line, 1 minute intervals, dogs screaming and you're off. Up the hill and then the 2 mile downhill where the fastest hit 30mph, whilst overtaking the slower teams that have been drawn ahead of you, all the way to the finish.

If you have had a good day Saturday you won't have anyone to overtake 2nd day as it's seeded, and fastest time in, means first out Sunday. So if you have the fastest time day one, happy days, barring an accident (more of that later) you will win... Aviemore.

This is the one race where there are no prejudices, all club members can enter (and **everyone** who races dogs in Britain is a club member) and you could be racing against anything up to 50 mushers.

Win that and you are the best.
And I wanted to be the best.
And I was determined to win!

Chapter 3

50 Shades of Yellow

They say an Inuit has fifty words for snow.

That's the white fluffy stuff that floats down from the sky and settles like icing sugar.

Well today, here in Meribel, the posh part of The French Alps, the snow isn't white.

It's yellow. Fifty shades of yellow to be precise.

I wonder if the Inuit's have fifty words for that.

You see, from the back of a dog sled, on the runners of my brand new all singing and dancing Danler about to start my first race on snow, it's just that, yellow. Brown even!

Unless of course you're first off.

But here at the Trophie de Savoie, you had to be good to get that position; very, very good.

And I wasn't, I'm what they call a "Rookie", a beginner.

And yet, here I was wondering what I'd let myself in for, when I was rudely awoken from my daydreaming.

Cinq, quatre, trois, deux, une, allez!

And we're off.

My 4 dogs (Joker, Dansa, Cougar and Bandit) had obviously picked up more of the lingo than me, and as soon as they heard "allez", they shot off like the proverbial bat out of hell, hurtling towards the first turning some 200mts ahead. You either made that turning or, bon voyage, take the quick route to the bottom of the valley by going straight on and hope you survive the couple of hundred metres drop.

We made the turn.

Once round the corner, grinning my head off, I quickly settled into the run thinking "this is easy, don't know what all the fuss is about."

Then we hit the woods!

My heart sank, ahead of us was a narrow track going down through the forest which to me looked like a vertical drop. Surely they don't expect us to go down that. I must have taken a wrong turning somewhere; better stop and check just to be safe. This would be the right and logical thing to do and you'd expect a tried and tested lead dog to read my thoughts and conclude that "yes boss, that's the best solution"

Not a snowball's chance in hell.

Joker took one look at the drop ahead, and I swear I saw him glance over and wink at his lunatic son Dansa, and that was it, the pair of them shot down the trail, leading the equally mad pair, Cougar and Bandit down that bloody track at a speed that would have Senna quaking in his boots.

No problem, thinks I, just pull the brake levers and slow them down. It was at this point that the major difference between a sled and a three wheeled rig finally entered my tiny brain. You have no brake levers on a sled, you have a foot brake. "Shit where's the bloody lever to stop this thing?" was, I think, the phrase that entered my head. Followed rapidly by "I'm going to kill myself," when I realised some idiot had forgotten to untie the bungee holding it upright, and it was firmly held tight. The idiot of course being yours truly.

"Joker STOP!" you bloody lunatic, slow down!"

Well you might as well have tried to turn back time (and at this point why did that record of Cher's enter my head?) than try and stop Joker and his gang. This was what they were born to do and, there I was, hanging on to a handlebar attached to two sticks and cursing why I'd ever entered this damn race, whilst the 4 of them did a very good impression of the driving of a bobsleigh down the Cresta run.

On and on we went bouncing off every banked turn trying to steer when the other obvious difference between sleds and rigs finally rammed home. You don't have a front wheel to steer you like a bike. Sure they both have "handlebars" but on a sled, handlebar is a very loose term, it's what you hold and LEAN into to make the turn. God how I wished I'd had a practice day on a sled, which is ironic because He was the only one who could have helped now, I was going to die.

STOP!

"Please stop Joker I promise I'll give you extra food and a warm bed indoors every day from now... just please stop!"

And then the miracle happened (thank you God!) we started to slow.

My prayers had been answered, the trail was now flat.

Flat... I'd made it, and, more importantly, alive and in one piece, and back in control.

The scenery changed, the speed changed, I started to enjoy myself. The sled and dogs, with me driving, started to glide along on the deep and crisp and even snow (I'm sure I've heard that before, sounds familiar), the sun was shining, the sky was bright blue, not a cloud to be seen, Daffodils blowing in the breeze (ok so that bit's made up but you get the picture) I'm thinking this is the life. "Bit more experience and I'll be entering The Iditarod."

Divvy!

Saw the ½ mile marker flag, signalling the end of the race was in sight, and I started to relax, smile even, I'm home.

Double Divvy!

Wallop!

"What the hell happened?"

I'm lying on the snow, sled on its side, me tied to it, and 4 dogs frantically trying to drag me and it to the finish line.

(Where did it all go wrong? Pride as they say comes before a fall.)

Well as I'd been gliding along doing my Wordsworth impersonation, I hadn't seen that the French, don't you just love them, had cunningly put a nasty little rise into the final part of the trail. To be fair they had warned you of a problem ahead, a yellow flag, universal (in husky racing anyway) notice of a hazard ahead. Me, in my daydreaming mode hadn't seen it, and was now suffering the consequences.

A quick glance back and I realised in my fuddled state what had happened. The trail had gone over a small hump, and immediately turned right. I'd expected it to go straight on. So I did .The dogs didn't. They turned, I and the sled flew, for a bit anyway. Then the gang line twanged tight, I performed a rather ungainly swallow dive and went head first into the snow.

My many years' experience of racing on rigs had taught me never to let go, and luckily this had kicked in, and before I could think what to do, I realised I'd flipped the sled upright onto its runners, and was now nonchalantly driving the team to the finish line, much to the admiration of the only spectator, an old French man, who greeted it with clapping and a rousing chorus of "chapeau, chapeau" (their equivalent of bravo), thinking I was some kind of stunt man.

Not daring to look back in case I'd spoil it for him when he saw the look of sheer desperation on my face, I called to the dogs "all the way home", and we crossed the line like seasoned pros. Phew!

There I was greeted by a mate who had finished just in front of me, Keith (he eventually came 2nd overall).

"How'd you find it?"

"Great, no problem."

"Come off at all?"

"Little mishap ½ mile back, that's about it."

And so that was it. My first day's racing in the Alps, on a sled, only 3 miles but I'd finished and in one piece.

I was a proper musher.

And then I thought about home.

Today was the 4th January 2003, and in Runcton, Chichester, I had left behind Cherry, my partner to care for, and Fly with her 3 new-born pups, Pepper, Detroit and the dog I was to eventually keep, Gun, in order to follow my dream and compete abroad, with my own dogs, on the Holy Grail for British mushers, Snow.

This had been an obsession with me for the past year, ever since I'd heard about it from two mates who had competed in it the previous year, John and Shane.

I was determined to go, but really needed someone to go with me, share the driving, etc. Immediately thought of Cherry, and broached the subject over a glass or two of wine as I thought rather naively, she would at least consider it.

"Cherry, how do you fancy a two week holiday in France this January. I'll pay and we could have such fun, different place each day, meal in a different restaurant each night. This could be the trip of a lifetime."

"Sounds great, why January and what about the dogs..."

At this point the penny dropped, she nearly choked on her wine and struggled to get some coherent words out, but the gist was as I remember. No get stuffed, I've had enough of your boys' weekends to last me a lifetime. Find someone else!

It was worth the try.

So, I phoned up a mate, Fred. When we were at a race meeting in Wareham the previous year we'd met up with John and Shane and they told us about the race they were going over to France the following week to compete in. On a whim both of us said we'd join them the next year.

But Fred being Fred, didn't have enough money to finance his own team, so the deal I now put forward was he paid all the fuel and toll costs, and I would supply him with 3 dogs (to make a 4 dog team with his own lead dog Wanda, Fly's litter sister) and pay the tunnel costs.

Obviously he said yes with the proviso that he could borrow my old wooden sled.

Me, I didn't mind, I had a brand new Danler to ride.

This was the sled of the moment, guaranteed to make you go faster, with its new style, removable runners and fold up design. Cost me a fortune, but at least I would look the part.

So it was now day 2 and I was in the start chute again, on my Danler, raring to go with my new found confidence.

The course had been lengthened to 5 miles as snow had fallen overnight, covering the parts of the trail that had been bare the day before.

We were also now being seeded on time finished the day before, so I was out middle of the pack; 15th out of the 30 entrants.

The race was unusual in that, to save time, you started the race in pairs, and between you, whoever got to the first bend in front was allowed to take the lead, thereby avoiding a potential crash.

I had decided the night before that I was going to hang back and let the team next to me take the lead, but my competiveness got the better of me once I saw him and his dogs. I reckoned they weren't a patch on mine, so once the flag fell and the dogs heard "Allez" we shot off taking the corner with aplomb, leaving the guy in my wake. And that's the last I saw of him.

Flying along I was starting to think I might make the podium, when we entered the tree lined downward white knuckle ride of yesterday. No problem, did it yesterday, just do the same. And we did until about half way down and disaster. Another team had stopped, on the narrow trail. And that's when I realised I wasn't as good as I thought I was. I tried to steer around him, Joker took the team as far across the narrow trail as possible, but the weak link was me and I smashed into the resting sled, taking out the musher, and releasing the hook holding his team.

Off they went down the trail, leaving me with a disgruntled French guy, holding his injured leg, and giving me a load of verbal's (I understood enough French to catch "Merde" by then).

Realising he was achieving nothing by bawling me out, he changed tack and quick as a flash, jumped onto the back of my sled runners, told me to chase (my French was improving rapidly now) and we headed off down the trail to find his team waiting for us at the bottom. Waiting! Couldn't believe it, mine would have been in Switzerland and freedom by now. But there they were, and without a word to me, he jumped off, muttered a load of, I presume comforting, words to his dogs, remounted his sled and disappeared into the distance without a backward glance. Charming, he could at least have offered to pay me for the lift.

So taking his cue, I called "allez" (when in Rome, etc.) and cruised home without further incident, never to see the guy again. Never did find out what happened and why he didn't make the rest of the race, but I'd now moved up a place. Maybe that's the way to get that place on the podium?

2 days down, 6 more to go.

What else could go wrong?

Next up was Peisey Nancroix and I found out soon enough.

Here the tension and excitement really got to the dogs, so much so that on the stake out chain Cougar bit Bandit on the leg, doing enough damage to render him useless for the next 2 days. Decided to go with 3, and didn't regret it one bit. Ok it was hard going up the hills with 3 and I was overtaken by the 2 teams who started 2 minutes behind me, but, and this was the important bit, within about 50mts of the crest of the hill. Once I could reach that it was downhill for the remaining 2 miles. And then we would fly. The 2 teams who'd just overtaken us were travelling down the hill, side by side when they heard me screaming to move over, both looked behind in time to see Joker take the team and sled through the tiny gap that had opened up for us, the 2 guys being so surprised they both fell off, remounted and then gave chase. 4 dogs against 3 shouldn't really be a competition, but Joker was no ordinary dog, he'd set the fastest time in Britain some 5 years earlier and now he had the opportunity to use that speed again. The downhill at Meribel was like a walk in the park compared to this. Admittedly my technique was crap as the French guy told me as we crossed the line, but it was good enough to beat him. And then I spoiled it, I fell off crossing the line looking back to grin at the two guys. But I didn't care, I was happy.

The next day the dogs really felt the strain of the previous day's exertions and though good, couldn't quite match that special run. Come back Bandit, all is forgiven. And he would. The next day was a rest day after 4 days hard racing.

Thursday saw us at St Gervais, Mont Blanc.

Here the French organisers really showed their sadistic side, with a real killer of a course.

At the Mushers meeting (each day you have a meeting to explain the course) which was in French and which did not cater for the other nationalities present, 6 Brits. 4 Dutch and 4 Czechs, it was explained that this was a very tough trail, with some very hairy turns to negotiate once the summit had been reached. This we noted was greeted by some very agitated Gaelic mutterings and throwing about of arms. The French were not happy. You didn't need an interpreter to understand those gestures. This resulted in three of our guys Fred, Shane, and Dougie, scratching from the day's race, leaving only me, Keith and John to race that day. And for the first time ever, I wore a crash helmet, and I needed it. A belated thank you Fred for plonking it on my head with; "you're going to need this".

The race started ok, albeit needing cramping irons to get you up the slope, under the ski lifts, and then after reaching the top, travel along the nice wooded ridge, and then the downhill run. What goes up comes down. Never a truer word has been said. The organisers had just cut switchbacks in the snow to get us back down the hill. Sleds were tumbling all over the place as the dogs took the turns at full speed and the sled was whiplashed around after them. It was carnage, broken sleds, runaway teams, injured mushers; the lot. Somehow I got back home safely, coming off countless times, not really counting as I was too busy picking myself up out of snowdrift after snow drift to care.

The next day saw the inevitable consequences, as 40 French mushers who were due to race in their following week's national championships, decided enough was enough and packed up and went home.

Belatedly, the organisers saw the error of their ways and reversed the course. This had the effect of nullifying the switchbacks but added a new problem. How to get the teams back down to the original starting point, which was in real life, the finishing line for the regular skiers. Solution, put up some barrier fencing to make you turn (The red plastic stuff you see round excavations everywhere in Britain.) and this coupled with a marshal waving you to slow down, appeared to work. It did in my case as we hurtled across the line without coming off once. Unfortunately we didn't all make it. That honour went to John, who taking his 8 dog team too fast, turned the sled over and finished the final 100mts being dragged face down across the finish line to, not sympathy, but howls of laughter and abuse from his mates; us!

By now I was up to 7th and that's where I finished overall after the final two days racing at La Grande Bernard – one a spectacular night rally where I rode most of the race in the dark after my lights failed, and the final day's racing, a mass start of 40 odd teams all galloping along a flat field to get to the first turning and the inevitable narrowing of trails that signalled chaos. If you imagine the Grand National, approaching Becher's Brook, that will give you some idea of the scene. Me, I held back, missed the inevitable mass pile up, finished the race and competition without incident, got my souvenir lumberjack shirt (no medals, certificate or anything remotely saying you'd competed) and headed back to Britain to decide what to do about the three pups Gun, Pepper and Detroit.

Chapter 4

Gun: A Year in the Life

I'd returned home to a well done from Cherry and a very pleasant surprise. She wanted to keep the black puppy, Gun.

This had me totally confused. I practically had to beg her to let me have Fly. "She needs a home" I said "She's Joker's daughter so she'll fit in and she will be the last dog I'll ever want, honest, no more, the last". Pathetic eh?

But it worked, she caved in.

Which was huge, given that Raider was supposed to be my last dog. I'd even written a letter to Cherry telling her that if she let me have Raider, he would be my last dog, and I wouldn't get any more. She still has that letter, and sarcastically produced it when I brought home Dansa (Joker's 8 week old son) 2 years later.

"But he's Joker's son, he needs a home and look, he's pure white. We've always wanted a pure white dog, and it means I'll be able to run a 6 dog team now. I can be a proper musher. And he will be the last dog I get. No more, the last."

She caved in again. (*More like gave up!*)

There's that American expression "3 strikes and you're out" so...

I was not about to go for a fourth try at the "it's the last dog routine". Reluctantly, I was resigned to selling all the pups. It had not been a planned mating, the money would come in handy after my French adventures, and I already had a 6 dog team. Besides, he wouldn't fit in, the age gap would be too big. Di Maggio, Cougar and Bandit would all be 10 by the time he was 1 year old. Joker would be getting on, 8 and a half. No I didn't need another dog. I was trying to persuade myself.

And then...

"What do you mean you want to keep him, are you nuts?"

"His name is Gun and we are keeping him, no arguments. You can sell the other two, but he stays, comprende?"

Now this was a totally unexpected turn of events

During the trip home, I had been rehearsing in my mind how I could persuade Cherry to let me keep the pups.

"They'll make a brilliant 3 dog team, a team to win Aviemore."

"You can't really split them up, Fly will be devastated."

"We have the room here, and these will be the last dogs I'll ever want."

Didn't think the last one would wash, but I had high hopes for the other two, so to be handed a new pup without any argument I decided not to push my luck any further.

So, Gun, welcome to the family.

Now all I had to do was find homes for the other two, Pepper and the big male Detroit, and decide on a suitable prefix (registered kennel name) for the three of them.

I wanted a name with a connection to my home town Birkenhead, and it had to be short and sound "cool" as the youth of today say (nicked from us in the sixties, but let them have their dream). As a kid I used to go to watch our local football team "Tranmere Rovers". Their greatest player was a local lad "Dixie Dean" who after he was transferred to Everton FC managed to score what still stands as a record to this day, 60 goals in a season. I met this legend once as a young kid, my mum knowing him very well. And just up from their ground was a small park that as kids we used to knock around in.

The name... ARNO.

Arno's Gun, sounded cool to me.

Duly presented it to the Kennel Club for registration, and it was rejected.

The reason? Arno is the name of Italy's major river (geography was never my strong point) and place names like that are not allowed as KC registered names.

Well I wasn't going to be deterred and with what I still think was a flash of inspiration, I Franglasized the name. Everywhere in France it's either Le or La, and with the addition of an "h" to make it look better it became "Leahrno". Sent the forms off again and hoped.

"Your application for the name has been accepted and we enclose the registration forms for Leahrno's, Gun, Detroit, and Pepper."

I was over the moon.

Now all I needed was to find homes for Pepper and Detroit.

And then I had a light bulb moment.

I remembered a young girl who had borrowed my old leader, Labi, to run at Aviemore in the juniors a few years back. She'd grown up a bit by the time I ran into her again in January 2000, when I was running 6 dogs and she handled for me. She also said that she was after getting a team together and was now a mother. She'd grown up quick, and I said I would contact if and when I bred a litter.

So I picked up the phone and called her up at her home near Inverness, offered her Pepper and Detroit and practically had to stop her from getting in her car to come and get them there and then.

"Stacey they won't be ready to leave their mother until, at the earliest, 16th February, so come down then." And she took me at my word, literally as on the 16th February, she and her little sister, Tori turned up on my doorstep in Runcton, Chichester, having driven the 650 miles overnight from Beaulieu Scotland. If nothing else they were keen!

Gave them both some well-deserved breakfast and introduced them to the pups. The big brown male Detroit, and his smaller sister, the brown and white piebald, Pepper. They fell in love with them immediately, the pups slobbering and wagging their tales furiously when they picked them up for the first time and I prepared to say goodbye.

Feeling both happy and sad Cherry and I waved farewell to the pups as the car made its way down our lane on the long journey back to Scotland.

Chapter 5

Training Begins

It's at this point in a young pup's life that small things make big impressions, and these lessons are quickly learnt and stick.

When Cherry and I lived in our first house, a maisonette in Lewes, we didn't have a garden, so having a dog as a pet was out of the question. Growing up in Birkenhead I'd been surrounded by dogs, cats, rabbits, guinea pigs, pigeons, in fact anything I managed to "find" and bring home as a stray, much to my parents' dismay. Trying to convince your mum that "honest, I found this lamb in Storeton Woods. Can I keep him?" was never going to be believed, and a long trip back to the farmer's field to put the lamb back in with its mother was the end of my "finds". I never repeated that again. But glancing through the local rag "The Friday Ad" I saw what I'd been searching for. Years previously Cherry had owned a pure black cat, which had passed away before I met her, and there on the page staring out at me was the ad "Free to good homes black and white kittens. Male and Female"

I should have looked at the ad more closely, as upon arriving at the farm I was greeted by what it said on the tin, black and white kittens. Not, black kittens and white kittens.

But, one of them, a big male, took my eye. I left with a "black" kitten. Ok it had a bit of white on it, but Cherry wouldn't notice, would she?

She did.

"That is not a black kitten, it's black and white. Do you think I'm blind?"

"Ah but he's lovely, and it's only a bit of white."

"He's got a big white chest and legs, he's going back. You're not palming that off on me."

And then "Baggins" as we were to name him, strolled over, brushed himself against Cherry's leg, purred, and she melted. He'd found his forever home.

About a year later, we put the Maisonette up for sale and I got Cherry a Cairn Terrier, "Potter" to keep Baggins company in the new garden that belonged to the house that we had bought, just outside Chichester, West Sussex.

All this of course was "brownie" points for my ultimate goal.

I wanted a Siberian Husky!

But what I wanted, what I really, really wanted was a wolf, but a "sibe" was the next best thing.

A wolf?

Let me explain.

It all started innocently enough with a trip to Chester Zoo, summer of 1970. Me and three mates were bored that day, and on a whim decided to go to the zoo, 15 miles away. None of us could drive, didn't even have a car, but you could go by local transport. Between us we had just about enough money to catch the local Crossville bus to the zoo, but not enough for the entry fee. Being resourceful "scousers" that was never going to be a problem. We got off the bus the stop before the entrance and used our complimentary passes to get in. We'd discovered a way to get in free the previous year.

We climbed the back fence.

Worked every time and we strolled into the Zoo, past the Antelope enclosure and soon mingled with the rest of the crowds.

Now around some of the enclosures were canals to keep the animals in, and young scousers out, but they were also packed full with fish, Roach. And this was the real reason we had come to the Zoo. Not to see the animals as most normal kids do, no we came to FEED the animals. Specifically the sea-lions.

We'd brought some fishing tackle with us, and soon had about a dozen large roach.

Walking over to the sea-lion enclosure, we became a hit with the tourists as we unofficially fed the seals. We were having a great time until we saw the approaching keepers. They were arriving for the Seals' official meal time. We disappeared pronto. Laughing, at what we thought was a great prank, we set off to explore the rest of the zoo. And there in one of the cages was a big dog... a wolf. Well it looked like a wolf, but with the keepers now having caught up with us we again had to make use of our complimentary passes and leave the Zoo the same way we entered; climb the fence and scarper, quick.

With no money left, it was a long walk home, but the experience stayed with me.

I wanted a wolf.

Now it was time for my "wolf".

Only you need a permit and a big enclosure for one of those. So, get the next best thing, a "lookalike".

Siberian Huskies had been imported into this country in the early 70's and one of the first people to own one was a lady called Jenny Manley. She owned "Howling Dog Kennels" in Fawley, down by the New Forest, about an hour's drive away from where we now lived. Decided to go down and look at these dogs, knocked on the door, and no answer. She was out. Not to be deterred, Cherry and I walked around the side of the property and peered over the fence.

That day changed my life forever.

Looking back up at us, completely silent, were a litter of 7 black and white Siberian puppies. I stood mesmerised. They never made a noise, just looked, and that image has stayed imprinted in my mind.

More than ever, I wanted a Siberian, and 3 months later I had my wish.

Jenny handed over a grey bundle of fluff. My first Siberian. Hustler.

Potter and Baggins, being roughly the same size, had by now formed a great friendship which lasted a lifetime, so when I brought Hustler home at 8 weeks old, I really didn't know what to expect. Every book you read tells you that Siberian

Huskies and cats don't mix, and you really shouldn't try keeping both.

I was about to find out if that was true or false.

Putting Hustler on the ground, Baggins casually wandered over to the equally inquisitive pup. He was all sweetness and light, no hissing no snarling. Great!

And then all hell let loose.

Baggins whacked Hustler across the nose with his claws extended, Hustler screamed, Baggins departed; job done. For the next couple of months Baggins used poor Hustler as his own personal punch-bag, even Potter got in on the act, dragging him around the garden and making his life a misery. But Huskies grow very fast, and soon he was too big and heavy for his transgressors. And then life became good for them all. Behind our house were some fields, and soon the locals had the unusual sight of a Cairn Terrier, a Siberian Husky, and a black and white cat, all off lead, going for their daily walks. The walks eventually led us to the pub, where we all enjoyed a drink, and the dogs got biscuits from the barman. We could usually have a couple of drinks before Hustler's stomach told him it was dinner time, he rose up from his place under the table, howled, we left, joined Baggins in the car park (he was tee total and wouldn't come in the pub), and made our way back home again where they were all fed and put to bed, all together in the kitchen.

Baggins, however never let sentiment get in his way, and continued this treatment to all our new pups, with the result that he was never once molested by the Huskies. When they were sometimes let out en-masse for a gallop round our large garden in Runcton, he would quite happily wander amongst them without the faintest sign of anxiety or fear. If anything, it was the Huskies that showed signs of respect, by kowtowing to this 10lb bundle of fur, teeth and claws.

And it was not just puppies he meted out the flashing claw treatment to.

In October 94, Steve Radburn had phoned me, and asked if I wanted to buy DiMaggio's litter brother "Cougar" who was now a one year old. Steve had refused to sell me him as a pup and offered me Bandit instead. His reason was he wanted to keep a male from that litter and he chose Cougar. It turned out that Cougar had grown too much, had a completely different "gait" (stride pattern) to the rest of his pack and was now surplus to requirements. Of course I said yes and went up to Coventry to meet his wife and said dog. But I was in for a surprise. He was totally underweight, (Steve liked his dogs lean) and very nervous.

So it was with apprehension that I brought him into the house that first night to give him a big feed and a bed for the night. As I entered I walked past the couch, not seeing Baggins lying there. But he saw him, out came the flashing right paw, which Mike Tyson would have been proud of and Cougar's nose exploded in streaks of blood. This was followed by a huge yelp and me being dragged to the end of the room, where a large chair came to his rescue. There he hid and began to lick his wounds, staying there for the next four days. Baggins had made his mark yet again.

Now at 16 years old Baggins was about to meet his "next victim".

Having separated Gun from his mum Fly, we let him have a little wander around the garden, before calling him over, another major part of his training, the recall, having already started. Over he came, bounding along, falling head first over the dwarf wall into the path of the waiting cat.

Baggins didn't flinch, as befitting a cat of his age and stature.

We waited to see what would happen next. After all it had been 5 years since he'd last given his special welcome to a pup, Dansa, and maybe he'd mellowed in his old age.

Gun, of course, had no idea. He came happily to his name and prepared to greet this strange looking "dog" when out came the right paw, claws extended, and "Gun" had his coming of age tribal scar.

Baggins wandered off to find his food bowl, whilst Gun whimpered (screamed really) until we let his mum, Fly, out to give him comfort and calm him down.

Now reading this, it seems cruel to put the pups through this procedure. Maybe to some people's eyes it is. But, the Siberian Husky really does have a fearsome reputation when it comes to cats, and would quite readily kill.

Baggins, in his own way, ensured that that would never be his fate. And in France where we now live, we have 6 huskies and 5 cats, all living in harmony (ok separated by weldmesh). But the dogs know which belong to us and will quickly bark and send packing any village cat that strays too near their pen.

Baggins had taught them well.

Next up was introducing Gun into the pen where he was to live.

This also can be a very risky business, introducing a small animal into a pen with fully grown adults. The prey drive with Huskies is a major problem. It's one of the reasons letting them run free causes so much controversy within the breed.

The vast majority of owners would not dream of letting their dogs off the lead, for fear of them running off, and either getting knocked over by a car, or worse, being shot by an irate farmer as it sees its "dinner"; a flock of sheep grazing in a nearby field, and attacks.

The solution, which seems to be beyond most owners' comprehension, is don't let them off anywhere near temptation, and teach them to come to their name. Simple really.

I've lost count of the number of times I've heard "if I let him off he'd never come back" as the owner is holding a fully grown Sibe straining at the lead as it watches other breeds of dog happily playing in an open space.

Any dog that has been kept on a lead all its life, if suddenly released is going to run.

Any dog that is suddenly released and has not been taught to come back as a pup, is a disaster waiting to happen.

This little bit of knowledge for some reason causes outrage with Siberian owners, who seem to think they own a totally uncontrollable wild animal.

Every Siberian I have owned (18) has responded to its name and has come back when called.

Six of those dogs, Hustler, Cassie, Labbi, Joker, Cougar, and Angel, I have regularly walked off lead on beaches, footpaths, reconnoitering new trails, knowing they would come to a recall.

Angel, who at 12 years old, is now too old to race, has a 3 mile walk 4 times a week in our local Forest at Mervent, in the Vendee, prior to me running Django, Bear and Reef with the Quad. And this can sometimes be in pitch black when I've forgotten my torch. And she comes back every time sometimes so quietly that I've found myself still calling for her when she's been at my side all the time, I just haven't looked.

But I digress.

I opened up the pen and put Gun and Fly in with Magi, Bandit and Raider, all fully grown adult males, and waited.

Gun was greeted like a long lost mate, all of them licking and knocking him over with boundless glee. No doubt the presence of a very watchful Fly helped, and soon I was able to leave them. Then it was a case of watching and trying not to laugh, as the adult dogs tiring of being chased around the pen, tails being bitten, found refuge on the raised platforms all Siberians love, whilst this little fat bundle of fur tried to join them, but was not yet big enough to make the leap.

Never mind, he'd settled in and we left him for the next couple of hours before the next big test.

Meal time.

All the dogs were fed mainly meat in separate bowls, around 6 pm every night.

They all had their own places in the pen where they liked to eat, and also the bowls to be placed in the correct order. I'm sure the writers of "The Big Bang Theory" based the character Sheldon and his quirky manner on Siberians' attitude to change. The bowl has to go down in the same place every time and in the right order, because the dogs are sitting waiting in their preferred spot. Do it differently and they panic, to the point if you put the bowl even 3 feet away they will not touch it but wait for their bowl to be put next to where they are waiting. I can just see Sheldon in them and his "today is Monday, we have oats on Monday , not Shreddies" as Leonard tries to change his diet. Watch the programme, it really sums Huskies up. Creatures of habit, which I have used to my benefit numerous times.

However, a young puppy: Gun, would not have this wired into his brain yet, and he was about to learn another important bit of training.

Do Not Pinch Food!

Magi as befitting his status as Alpha male was always fed first, followed by Fly, Bandit and the "youngster" Raider. So without giving it much thought, I put Maji's bowl down, and moved onto Fly, when an almighty scream split the air, followed by a fat little bundle, Gun, frantically licking yet more blood from his nose. Quickly put the other two bowls down, and then picked the little one up, put him and his food bowl in a safe corner, where his hunger got the better of him, and he quickly scoffed the lot.

But a second and very important lesson had been learnt.

Do not try and nick another dog's food, and especially not the boss's, even if he is your dad. A Siberian's food belongs to him and him alone.

We were now going to the training ground around three times a week, Fly having restarted training 6 weeks after giving birth. But with the other two pups now departed, Gun was now coming with us. He would sit in the truck while the adults did their run, and yell until they came back, not happy to be parted from his mum. Now it was time for his first "run".

You initially walk a pup on a lead attached to the tug line on the harness. That's the theory anyway. Gun, as I was to discover, was a very quick learner. He'd obviously been watching the older dogs, and as soon as his feet hit the deck, took off down the trail, minus me still holding the unattached lead.

Now you'd think that an 12 week old fat pup wouldn't be that fast.

You'd be wrong!

Gun flew down the trail oblivious to everyone and my frantic calls trying to get him to come back. Nothing for it but to run down the trail and try and catch him. So off I went, struggling in heavy boots and full wet weather gear (it was raining), to the sound of raucous laughter ringing in my ears from my training partners, Hughie and his grandson Carl.

Took me about 200mts to catch the little sod, and quickly put the lead on him, intending to walk him back to the waiting truck. He decided otherwise, I felt a tug on the lead and we were off again, me running behind and him galloping for all he was worth.

The trail now bore right and he followed it with me calling out the command to turn right "gee". Another 300mts, the trail turned again, we turned right, gave him the command again, he took it and then it was a straight run home of another 300mts, with both Hughie and Carl calling Gun home. He immediately picked up the pace, me struggling to keep up and hanging onto the lead, when he came to a grinding halt at Hughie's feet.

As ever, Hughie had some treats out and Gun readily wolfed the lot down, before I put him back in the truck with his mum and dad.

Me, I was busily gulping down water and trying to catch my breath. I had not expected to run a fast kilometre at all, especially in totally unsuitable clothing. It wasn't as if I was totally unfit, I could still run a mile in 6.30 minutes, but I didn't expect to have to do it that day. But I was bursting with pride. Gun had showed a tremendous attitude for running, and the future as they say "looked Rosy".

The next few months followed the same routine, trying to get Fly back up to racing speed. March 2nd we entered a race about 30 miles from home, and paired with Joker, Fly duly delivered the win, 10 weeks to the day after giving birth, amazing!

In the meantime I was still running behind Gun, and I have to admit I was not enjoying being dragged around Selhurst Park (Goodwood) by my rapidly growing and increasingly more powerful, bundle of fluff. I was still quite fit, only weighed about 11 stone soaking wet, and at my best ran 10 miles in 58mins. Now that's not a bad time, but it only equates to about 10 miles an hour. That's positively pedestrian to a Husky, who'll quite happily run at that speed all day, and in freezing conditions pulling a weighted sled. As a further comparison, Cougar, my big male doesn't break into a gallop until the speed hits 13mph. The time had come to start rig training for young Mr Gun!

As all my racing dogs were much too fast for him, I turned once again to the dog who had been my stalwart over the years, Pierre Labbatt, other known as Labi.

This was a dog bred from Hustler and my female Cassie.

Although from mainly show lines, he had surprised everyone by becoming a very good sled dog, him and his litter sister Gabbi and their father Hustler, providing me with my first victory on 7th March 93 at Ashley Heath, Dorset. He won his last race in 6 dog in Clocaenog, North Wales, December 99 cutting his feet in the process, and then promptly retired himself. He was 9 years old. From that day on if you went into the pen with a harness he would hide in his box and flatly refuse to come out. No amount of coaxing would persuade him otherwise, so that was it. He decided that he didn't like cut feet, had done his bit and had now earned his r and r. Full stop.

However, he did like to go for his daily walk with me down the gravel track at the bottom of our road, us living in a semi-rural area. I figured that if I walked him and Gun down the lane together, there was every possibility I could harness the both of them up, hook them up to the rig and run them the 500mts back to our house.

To make absolutely certain of this plan working, I needed someone else to drive the rig, whilst I was out front encouraging what after all would be a momentous occasion in Gun's sled dog career, his first run on a rig.

You have to be very careful at this stage, as one false move, an unpleasant experience can put off a dog for life, and a ruined sled dog.

For the past couple of months a young lad called Ewan, had been coming to help me train the dogs. He knew them, only weighed about 7 stone and would be ideal. He readily agreed when I asked him. So on Saturday 19th April 2003, with his mum and dad, Cherry and half the neighbourhood watching, he stood on the rig, I called out "hike" from my position 50mts up the road, and they shot off. Labi responded as I hoped he would, leaned into the harness and pulled, Gun, bless him, didn't miss a beat, matched Labi stride for stride and raced to catch me giving it all I could to get back to the house before they caught me up. And they nearly did, Gun outrunning a tiring 12 year old Labi, before I stopped them both outside the pen to give them both a big hug and Labi, his reward, a freshly cooked pork hock. This he gently took from my hand, pushed open the back door gate, made his way to the rear of the garden were he stayed till he ate the lot, bone and all.

Gun, meanwhile was still full of energy, and upon putting him back in his pen, proceeded to chase his mum until a sharp nip put him back in his place with a contented Fly no doubt reminding her son of the old adage "let sleeping dogs lie".

Me, I was beaming like the proverbial Cheshire cat. Fly and Maji had produced what was rapidly becoming obvious to everyone, a pure sled dog that could run. I was ecstatic.

But it didn't last long. I looked over to the other pen and out of the corner of my eye, noticed Hustler lying quivering on the ground. I rushed in and picked him up, and it was immediately obvious that he was not well. He was having trouble breathing, and was stumbling when he tried to walk.

Got him into the truck and drove as fast as I could to the vets, opened up the back door to the truck, and there was Hustler. Standing up wagging his tail and giving me his big grin.

Thinking he'd recovered, I turned around and drove straight back home, put him back in his pen, fed them all and bedded them down for the night. Little did I know, that was the last time I would see Hustler like that.

The next day was bright and sunny, and all seemed well with the dogs. Hustler was lying contentedly in the sun, as were all the rest of the pack.

Never really gave it much more thought until Cherry happened to mention that Hustler looked really cute, lying on a brick as he did the first day we brought him home as a pup, all those years ago.

Trouble was, he was in a coma.

I picked him up, brought him into the house, lay him on the carpet by the fire hearth, and stayed with him till he gently passed away in my arms at 4.am, Monday 21st April. He was 15 years and 10 months old.

I had him cremated 2 days later, on St Georges Day, 23rd April 2003.

And I didn't stop crying for weeks.

I was sitting in the garden a few weeks later when Baggins, who had recently gone blind, walked over to me and sat on my lap. Strange, he'd never ever done this before. He was and remained a very aloof cat all his life, as befitting his farm upbringing. When I'd taken him to the vets, they said I should put him down as his quality of life would be compromised by his blindness. I told them no thank you, and brought him home. He'd adapted well, but never ventured out again, until today.

I stroked him and talked to him and took him back inside. The next morning on the 8th May I came downstairs and found him curled up in his basket, dead. He was 17 years old.

I buried him under a tree were he used to sleep in the front garden, and the tears returned.

Chapter 6

Coming of Age

I had decided that one litter was enough for Fly and had her spayed at the beginning of April. She had now recovered and was "bouncing off the kennel walls." This was enough to get me in training mode again.

We made our way up to the training ground at Goodwood, the weather had cooled sufficiently after a sweltering May, and I was looking forward to running Gun with his mum at lead. I decided to put Cougar and Dansa at wheel and off we went. Gun ran the 1.4 mile course at a very fast pace and took all the turns perfectly dragging his mum round a couple of them as she was not listening to my commands, she was more interested in admiring the scenery after her operation.

Me, I couldn't believe what I was seeing, Gun was leading 3 of the fastest dogs in the country at 6 months old. Conventional Siberian wisdom will tell you that you don't put them in harness till they are about 8 months old, and then only for a short couple hundred metres run at most. Well Gun was proving that wrong, and he was running like a "pro".

As the weather was still hot, I'd started to take Gun to, horror of horrors, Ringcraft. I'd always struggled with this "sport". I couldn't and still can't understand the need for this "beauty parade". You wander around the ring with a load of other dogs, and the "Judge" decides the best dog. And usually, all the losers disagree with the result. Give me a race every time, fastest time wins, end of story.

But Hughie, my training companion, saw potential in Gun (he'd won a puppy class at Cruft's with his Sibe Logan), so we gave it a go. I say we, what really happened was I paid someone else to do the training for me as I watched. I just could not get the hang of prancing round the ring trying to control Gun to the satisfaction of the Judge. We both wanted to run!

But "we" persevered and eventually won a puppy class at a local show and I was persuaded by Hughie to enter the club Championship show being held that September at Windsor. Here despite Gun clearly being the best puppy in the ring (in my opinion) and being shown to perfection by an experienced club member (thanks Sarah) he was placed 4th... 4th! And that was to a dog with only half a tail. That was the end of Gun's showing career. The trail beckoned.

Up at Goodwood I'd already run Gun in August in an 8 dog team around the 2 mile loop and he looked fine. But now the real test was to come. The weather had cooled down and on Tuesday night on the 7th September at 8 months old that test was at hand. I was going to run him at lead in 4 dog with... Joker.

And he didn't fail – he bloody well *flew*.

Joker in November '97, had run lead on a mates "all conquering" 6 dog team (the best team Britain has seen) at a race I had organised at Head Down near Petersfield, and recorded a 21mph average speed over the 2.2 mile course, a record nobody has ever beaten. This mate, Neil, had also used Joker to win the British Championship 2 dog class the following year, so this was a real test, and Gun had passed with flying colours. He didn't look out of place at 8 months old against "the best lead dog of his generation" as Fred would write memorably about Joker years later.

Feeling really chuffed, I took all the dogs home, gave them some chicken carcasses as a reward and put them to bed, looking forward to the coming season. All was well.

But it wasn't. Again, fate kicked me in the teeth, and the consequences eventually proved disastrous.

I was now regularly running all 8 dogs using the quad.

We usually ran Tuesday nights and 2nd October would be just another run. But it wasn't.

As usual, Joker was put onto the lines first, basically because he could be trusted to keep the gang line taut and not turn around to investigate the other dogs. I'd once made the mistake of putting Joker at wheel and Raider at lead, and he'd promptly turned around and attacked Joker, Maji saw his chance and attacked Cougar, Dansa backed up his mate and attacked Maji, Fly bit whatever came within range of her mouth, and Gun just cowered in the dust hoping nobody would attack him. End of training run and harsh lesson learned. Always put Joker on first.

I had by now 7 dogs all hooked up and went back to get the last dog, Gun. And then I heard Hughie screaming at me. Running down the trail were Joker, Fly, Cougar, Dansa, and bringing up the rear Bandit. Looking at the remnants of the gang line it quickly became obvious what had happened. It had been bitten clean through. The culprit... Raider. It had to be him, Maji had no teeth.

Now normally you would be in a state of panic, 5 Siberians running free in the woods at night. But with Dansa and Joker in lead, I was surprisingly calm. Dansa was a very strong willed dog. Once he started a run, be it race or training, he would finish. You just could not get him to do anything else. He knew the trail and would run it WITHOUT commands and bring the team back to the truck. Trouble is, once there he would jump up and try and take the whole team back into his box. How was I so sure? You don't train Huskies without the odd mishap, and I'd come off a couple of times before and, without fail, the dogs instead of stopping, would just carry on regardless, rig bouncing along behind them, and complete the training run. And by the time I made it home, there they would be, half in half out of a box made to hold, at best, two dogs.

"Here's the plan Hughie, you go along the trail we ran on Sunday and catch up with them, I'll stay here in case they go a different way."

Off he went whilst I unhooked Maji and Raider and waited. It was pitch black by now and looking at my watch, I reckoned the team would soon be back, 10 minutes being about right for the 3 mile course. Almost to the minute I saw the tell-tale sets of glowing eyes gleaming in my head-torch lights.

"Phew you're home."

And then I looked, Bandit was missing.

Blind panic set in. Where was he?

And then another set of lights and Hughie turned up, carrying Bandit on the fuel tank of his Quad. And Bandit was battered and bloodied.

"Hughie what happened?"

"Caught up with them by the Pylon, and saw Bandit was being dragged. Put the quad in front to stop them and try to walk them back. Dansa would not stop pulling and I was getting dragged so I unhooked Bandit and let the rest go". Hughie, I should add, was into his late sixties by then, and I couldn't thank him enough for his actions. After giving Bandit a look over, we figured out what had happened. Because Gun was the last dog to be put on, he had a loose tug line next to him. He'd tripped over this, slipped and the rest of the team just carried on as normal, finishing the run pulling the "rig"... Bandit!

Gingerly we picked him up and put him on the front seat of the truck, Joker being resigned to the backseat, but not before giving his mate Bandit, a reassuring sniff.

Back home, after feeding and putting the rest of the team away, Cherry and I attended to Bandit's wounds. Luckily, and we were lucky, Goodwood is 90% grass trails. And they were the ones we trained on. And it had been raining lately. He'd been dragged, but that rain and grass had saved his life, he'd slid.

But he was out for the month and I never repeated that mistake again. The gang line was reinforced with wire!

So with a depleted team, we completed the first races of the season late October, placing 4th and 1st.

With races entered on the first three weekends in November, Gun's training was interrupted. I still had to get the others race fit, and those three weekends resulted in three first places, two thirds and one second.

And now it was time to train for Aviemore.

With all 8 dogs fit and raring to go I decided to really test Gun. Alongside Joker once more we tackled the longer 2.6 mile course at Goodwood and we stormed round.

Two days later, the same formation 4.4 miles and same result. I was overjoyed. 8 dogs fully fit and I only needed 6 for Aviemore and we were running the distance already. We might have a chance.

Gun was getting better and better, and more importantly, was holding his own. But I had noticed that the older trio, Maji, Bandit and Cougar, all now 10 years old, were at times starting to show just a sign that the speed was getting to them. But that was to be expected, 7 years for a Siberian is considered old, and 10 would be positively ancient. I would just play it by ear.

It was now nearly Christmas and time for what had turned out to be a bit of fun for the dogs. Cherry was based at a Garden Centre about ½ mile from where we lived. As this place had a large restaurant it was very well attended, and to bring in the clients they had a Grotto with their own Father Xmas on the two Saturdays before the big day. Cherry happened to mention that she had a fully-fledged Husky team, and so with Hughie we were roped in to be the equivalent of Father Xmas' reindeer transportation. We would hook up 8 dogs and bring him in on the back of his own sled (ok no snow so we used a quad). The big day arrived, the place was full of young kids and their mothers all looking forward to the grand entrance. And they got it. Into the car park the team arrived, led by, you guessed it, the pure white DANSA. Ok we didn't have any of the other names, but the kids didn't seem to mind. As soon as we stopped and let Father Xmas off, the kids swarmed over the 8 dog team, 4 of Hughie's dogs replacing 4 of my wilder ones.

It wasn't long before each of the kids had their favourite dog, proudly hanging onto the neck of their preferred choice. Which, in this day and age absolutely amazed both Hughie and I and of course Cherry. Here were kids as young as 6 months old hanging onto fully grown 55lb strange dogs, and nobody was panicking. We had no doubt that our dogs would be fine, we wouldn't have agreed otherwise. The Siberian Husky, if it's brought up properly is one of the safest breeds with young kids. Of course small furry prey are a completely different matter, but small kids, fine. And Gun was taking full advantage of the situation. His particular "fan" was a joy to watch. He was a small boy of about 3 years old and he had Gun eating out of the palm of his hand... literally. This little kid had a mince pie, and we all watched amazed as he had told Gun to "sit down". Gun to my amazement did as he was told. The little boy then took a bite from his pie, chewed it, bit off another bit, and gave it to Gun. He didn't snatch, just gently took it from "his mate". This carried on until the pie was finished, the little kid patted Gun, he gave him a big sloppy kiss, and they parted best of mates.

But back to training.

Fly was now running as fast as ever, having fully recovered from her operation earlier in the year. Gun was flying, Joker ditto. And on 27th December I had the best run with the 8 dogs of my life. Aviemore 6 here we come.

What's that phrase about not counting your chickens? Well it came home to roost.

Twice!

Cougar in his youth had had a toe amputated after a fight with his brother Magi. Now at 10 years old, he had started to favour that leg, and often came home slightly limping. The hard trails of Aviemore would do him no favours, so when he finished a training run over the Xmas period, I bit the bullet. Cougar was out of the team.

7 dogs left.

January 1st. Training run at Goodwood, all was fine until I took a look at Dansa. He looked like he was auditioning for the part of Quasimodo. His right eye was closed and he had a huge lump on his head. Trip to the vets on the way home, operation and 6 stitches next day. He now looked like he'd been 10 rounds with Mike Tyson. The vet said he'd pulled out a bit of wood that had become infected. How it got there I have no idea, but I had lost another dog for the team.

6 dogs left

Aviemore; 22 days to go.

I still had a team so I still trained, hard. Ok it was not my best combination, but we still had a chance.

Aviemore; 15 days to go

Dansa's wound had rapidly healed. Ok he still looked a mess, but his fur was growing back, and he wanted to run. Back in lead with Joker and it was as if he'd never been away. I had my team back.

Aviemore; 6 days to go.

Goodwood Sunday 18th January 2004.

Last training run before leaving for Scotland. Cougar was definitely being left behind. Joker and Dansa would be my leaders. Maji was going in at wheel. Fly would be at point. Gun would be next to her. It was now a straight choice for the last remaining spot right wheel next to Maji. Bandit or Raider? Bandit was now 10 years old and slowing down. Raider was 3 years younger and Maji's best mate (or so I thought). It was a no brainer. My 6 had been chosen.

Aviemore; 2 days to go.

Thursday 22nd January

I packed the 6 dogs into my pickup truck. Said goodbye to Bandit and Cougar, kissed Cherry goodbye and made my way up to the A27 by Chichester and the long overnight journey to Aviemore.

Aviemore; 1 day to go.

Friday 23rd January.

The draw for starting positions was made.

I was drawn second. Couldn't be better.

Aviemore; we're ready.

Chapter 7

The Dogs and Equipment

Although Aviemore is run by The Siberian Husky Club, the race is not just confined to that breed. There are four recognised Pure Bred Nordic dogs, in order of size – Alaskan Malamute, Eskimo/Greenland, Siberian Husky, and Samoyed. They all belong to the Spitz group of dogs and all use the generic term "husky".

This is not to be confused with the dog known as the "Alaskan Husky", which is a "Heinz 57", and can and often does look like your average mongrel. However, and this is a big however, the bloody things can run, and run, and often very, very fast. They as the name says, originate in Alaska, and are a culmination of years of careful breeding by "mushers" wanting to improve performance in the original Huskies. Mostly there is Siberian blood in there somewhere, along with pointers, greyhounds, various Norwegian hounds, in fact anything to improve stamina and speed. These dogs have taken over in the sport of Long and Mid distance racing on snow ranging from about 200 miles to the daddy of them all, The Iditarod.

Sprint racing, usually 30 – 50 miles (on snow) is dominated by varying breeds of hounds. These dogs run considerably faster than the four Nordic breeds, but have one major disadvantage. Apart from not looking the part, they are short haired. Now short hair and minus temperatures do not go together very well. These dogs are often housed in heated kennels, and are only brought out to train and race and then back inside to keep warm. Some sled dog eh?

However this trend for speed at any cost has now appeared in Britain, mainly in Scotland, and it's not unusual to go to a race meeting and see both hounds and huskies competing. Admittedly, the hounds only race against their own type, the "open" class, but it's a trend very much on the up.

Personally, I got into racing because of the Siberian, and that's where I'll stay. Fortunately there are more than enough like-minded souls around to keep the breed alive and kicking... for now. But I fear for the survival of this beautiful breed.

I have to admit though that despite the disadvantages of hounds, they do have one very compelling advantage over the Husky.

They can be trained like a normal dog.

The Siberian on the other hand is at the other end of the spectrum, he can and often does forget he's a dog.

The first time you set eyes on a typical Sibe you'll think of one thing only.

"Is that a Wolf?"

It's a question any owner will have heard a thousand times. And without doubt, there is a striking similarity in looks. If that was where the similarity ended you'd be fine. Unfortunately it doesn't.

If and when you go to buy a Sibe puppy, you'll be amazed at how good looking and gentle they are, a cute bundle of fun. You'll be told something along the lines of how good they are with people, but a danger to livestock and small furry animals... cats.

All of it good generic advice.

But this really is the Wolf in sheep's clothing.

And what you aren't told could lead to you having big problems.

1) Certain strains of Siberians have been selectively bred because of their willingness and attitude to running, mine are prime examples. After all who wants a slow sled dog if they are going to race? But this attitude boils over into their kennel life. Consequently, as they mature, some start to believe they are destined to be pack leaders. In effect the so called "alpha

male". Here the problems really do start. Those cute litter brothers, as they mature, (usually about 1 year old) now hate each other with a passion, a real and deadly passion.

I wasn't told about this but learnt the hard way. My first "true" running dog was Maji, and I had wanted two from the same litter. Steve Radburn the Breeder, said No he wanted to keep the rest of the litter. However a year later I was overjoyed to get a phone call asking if I still wanted the other male. Is the Pope Catholic? And 1 week later I collected "Cougar", Maji's litter brother. All was fine for the first 6 months, Cougar being very timid and shy. But it soon changed, and after a particularly bloody encounter, decided reluctantly to kennel them separately. They still argued through the fence though; Magi once ending up with his bottom lip being practically torn off, only for him to return the compliment and bite off Cougar's right toe two weeks later. And all this through four inch square weld mesh. Beware!

2) They have the memory retention of an elephant.

On the trail this can and sometimes does work in your favour. Once a lead dog knows the route of the trail, he can get you round without the required commands. This is great if you are out at night and your headlamp fails (Yes you guessed, it happened to me), because your trained leader will take all the required turns, and get you home safely. But, it's scary because although you both know the way, that little right hand bend that you take very easily, now in the pitch black becomes a tight hairpin that causes you to hang on for dear life, as your friendly lead dog just carries on regardless. He can see in the dark, and doesn't he let you know it. A very, very good and effective laxative!

3) The combination of memory retention and yearning to be Alpha Male, can cause major problems when hooking up your team ready to run.

All teams in this country are run in tandem (side by side). They are connected to a gang-line (central rope attached to the Sled/rig/quad) in two places. By a short lead (neck line) connected to each dogs' collar, and a longer line (tug line) connected to the rear of the running harness the dog is wearing. In this way with correct spacing, teams of up to 8 pairs (16 dogs) are successfully raced. In this way you have the power of the dogs channelled in a straight pull allowing you to run very, very fast along twisting narrow trails.

To do this successfully the paired dogs have to get on with each other.

If not... stand back and watch the explosion.

And this is where the memory retention comes in.

Not only do Sibes love running, settling "old scores" runs it a close second.

The "little buggers" (because that's what they are) remember every little argument they've had, and will wait for years if necessary to settle the score.

And this is where you have to be very careful at races, where out of necessity you need extra hands to take the dogs to the start line, where they are then hooked up to the rig. (On a sled it's much easier, you hook up with the sled anchor engaged and run them to the start line as a team, the so called Alaskan start.) So it is not a good idea to just ask the nearest passer-by to "take a dog to the start chute for us mate"

This is a God given opportunity for any Siberian worth its name to settle old scores, and frequently they do.

It's amazing how fast they can lunge at their "enemy" and inflict gaping wounds (usually to the legs) whilst the friendly inexperienced handler is idly chatting away to his mate. This had disastrous consequences for me, not once but twice, and both at... Aviemore.

Chapter 8

Equipment and Rules

Like most organisations, you can't just turn up at the venue and compete, you have the dreaded entry form to fill out and send to the race organisers. This can and often does cause panic for some of us, me included. I've lost count of the times I've missed the time deadline and had to sheepishly phone up the organiser and confess to not sending out the form. This is where being an "old timer" comes in handy, you know most of the race organisers, you've raced against them for years, so usually you can blag an entry. Not so at Aviemore, this is the one race where "being a name" cuts no ice. Because of the monumental organisation that goes into running the race, the cut-off date for registration is last day of November. No sob stories here, even one day late and you are out. No exceptions.

The registration form is however very simple to fill out. You give the names of your registered dogs, and pick the class you want to enter. A, B, C, D, E, which corresponds to, 8, 6, 4, 2, and 3 dogs. And that's the little bit of irregularity which can and often does confuse people. For years there were only the 4 classes, so logically A, B, C, D followed. But in 1999, due to the vast number of entrants who owned 3 dogs, a class was put on for them, and the next letter was E. It was very easy to mix up the classes at first and many a disgruntled competitor found he'd entered 3 dogs when he thought he'd entered 2 and vice versa. Oddly, I competed in the first 3 dog race at Aviemore, and if I say so myself I was a red hot favourite to win. But a puncture each day meant I finished in the position I'd come to know so well over the previous 3 years, 2nd. But that's another story.

The draw is made on Friday evening for starting order, and on Saturday morning before you can race, your rig and lines are inspected. The rig, has to be within certain size limits, but wheel size is up to personal choice. Most nowadays use 20 inch BMX wheels but it's not unusual to see the full size 26 inch versions being used. The vast majority of rigs are of the 3 wheel version, though there is a trend for the 8 dog competitors to use the much more stable 4 wheel version. And a major factor; there is no weight restriction. This often causes the incredulous looks on the first time spectator when they see 8 frantic huskies screaming in anticipation, being "hooked" up to what is really a frame on wheels. With good cause really, you may have the best disc brakes money can buy on your rig which will lock up and stop the wheels turning very effectively. **But,** and it's a huge but, it won't stop a full 8 dog team. They have the power to just drag the rig and musher all the way to the finish line and there is nothing you can do about it.

In France where I now live, they have minimum weights for the rigs in each class. Even in 2 dog the rig must weigh a minimum 30kgs. 8 dog goes up to 70kgs. And that will stop the team.

And that's the peculiar situation we have in Britain. All equipment is checked, but the two most important pieces of kit are not inspected. The dogs and the musher. No safety gear whatsoever is required for the musher, and no vaccinations are checked for the dogs. Again in France, vaccination records for each dog must be produced, verified by your Vet and each musher must have a medical check-up and documentation sent to the Club Secretary before she will issue you with a licence to compete. Rigs are not inspected. I think the French, for once, have their priorities right here.

Chapter 9

Aviemore 2004

The Race: B Class

I'd arrived bright and early for the start, 7am. Well I thought I was early, but by the time I rolled into the car park, literally every man and his dog was already there. The place was buzzing, the noise from over 1000 dogs "howling" in anticipation of the coming day's racing was deafening.

"You're in 6 dog aren't you Jim?" I was greeted by a marshal.

"Unfortunately Yes."

"Turn left then, there's still a place left next to Bruce"

"Thanks."

And with that I manoeuvred my truck into the car park, to be greeted by the usual derisory remarks.

"Afternoon."

"Sleep in did we, race started about an hour ago, you've missed your start."

The "mickey taking" had begun.

"What's the matter, couldn't afford the hotel so had to camp out all night in the cold, get a job!" I could give as good as I could get.

But I had things to do.

Walk and water the dogs, get the rig out and inspected, and then take it to the start line, and come back and have the morning's first cup of tea.

This part of the car-park had the food wagons, toilets and various trade stands and the all-important running order of the day. This was where the hub of interest was until the race started with 8 dog and then following in order 6, 4, 3, and 2.

Here I met my mate "Welsh John".

"Alright Jim. Had a look at the race order, you've got a real chance of winning."

"Let's have a look then."

Scanning the running order I was starting to believe, then I saw a name I didn't want to be there "Shane Murray".

I'd known and raced against Shane a long time. Even been racing with him in France the previous winter. And he had young dogs, and they were fast.

"Reckon you're wrong John, think Shane's got this one"

Maybe he did have the better team, but I wasn't about to make it easy for him. Until you finish, anything could and often did happen, I was living proof of that. No, I was going to give it my best shot, and went back to my truck to prepare to race.

I'd decided my team formation, and went over it again in my mind, Joker and Dansa up front. Gun and Fly next. Raider and Maji at wheel. I would boot Dansa as the trail was a bit hard and he dug in particularly hard when he ran up hills, a real power house. This is fine but meant he ran the risk of wearing down his nails to the "quick" on the first hill.

So I was ready, better have a cup of tea to calm my nerves. And another. Go to the toilet. Check the watch. Have another cup of tea. Check the dogs. Go to the toilet. On and on it went. Relentless.

"Jim, 10 mins till you're off," I heard Welsh John say.

"Fine, they're all harnessed, let's make our way to the start."

As we were in the near car-park it was only a relatively short "drag" by the dogs to the start chute. So my 6 "handlers" and I made our way to the start line. As we were off second, we made our way past the rest of the 6 dog competitors waiting their turn, and hooked up the dogs in their positions on the gang line.

"Go!"

"And next up is Jim Bryde from Chichester." The dulcet tones of Sarah Robinson announcing my arrival on the line.

"30 seconds to go."

"15 seconds."

"Good luck Jim."

"5, 4,3,2,1, Go."

And we're off.

And we're flying, Gun not phased at all. His very first race, hundreds of spectators lining the route, and he's flying. I'm on my way.

The first twisting bit of the trail goes by in a blur and I'm looking ahead to the coming hill. Not a problem, we storm up and begin to pick up speed. And there ahead, my mate Roy, the team that started 2 minutes ahead of us. We'd made up the time inside the first mile. We were motoring. Roy saw us coming and I really didn't need to call out "trail", (the signal to pull over to let a team overtake) he was already slowing down and pulling over for me.

"Go get 'em Jim," I heard as I flew past. And that was and still is the joy of running dogs. The vast majority of "mushers", recognise a better team, and will actively encourage them on, and are genuinely pleased for their success. It could be their turn next, dogs being at their peak for only three to four years and then the downward spiral. "Don't be nasty to people on the way up, you're liable to meet them on the way down" is a very apt phrase.

We should now have had an uninterrupted run down to the Loch, so I let the dogs have their head. I had no doubts about the rest of the dogs, but I kept a very close eye on Gun. There was a chance that the speed could "freak him out" and he'd put the brakes on. This is something you don't want. A frightened dog simply decides to stop. Unfortunately, the rest of the team doesn't, and the result is the pads get ripped off the dog. It is not pretty, blood everywhere, the end of your race and more importantly, a badly injured dog. I'd seen this happen a couple of times, and you need to be very attentive to minimise the damage.

But Gun was taking this all in his gigantic stride, and then we saw a team pulling over, ahead.

It was Dougie McPerson. "A" class had started earlier, and was 7 miles long, meaning twice round the trail for them. He had started some 20 minutes ahead of me and I had caught him on his second lap. Calling trail we stormed past and onto what I assumed would be a clear last mile and a half.

I was starting to enjoy this now, the dogs were running in perfect unison, Gun looked like he'd been there all his life and I was looking forward to crossing the finish line safely. And then up ahead, another team. Bruce Hall. This was the guy who'd given me my very first husky riding lesson all those years ago in Wales.

"Come on Bruce, you can make it, only one more hill to go and you're home" I shouted as we passed him. And then with the encouragement, his dogs picked up, and chasing me the final 400mts, we crossed the line within metres of each other. And there I was 1st, on the leader board. But would I stay there? My time was under 15 minutes, which was damn fast considering I had a 10 year old running, but I knew it wasn't fast enough. Still I waited, and waited and waited. It was looking good, I was still first on the leader board. I was starting to believe. Until I saw my nemesis appear over the final hill. Shane. He was flying and I knew the game was up, and I didn't need to look at the leader board. I finished the day in 2nd place, 34 seconds adrift.

Aviemore Day 2: Starting Chute 6 dog

"That was Shane Murray off. Next up Jim Bryde"

I had made my way to this point, trying desperately to install confidence in myself and the dogs. They, to give them credit, were raring to go. Gun was practically ripping the arm off his handler, desperate to get going. His attitude soon rubbed off on the rest of the team and we had a job to hear the commentary of the starter. The dogs were going ballistic, even Maji, who was usually as cool as a cucumber. Maybe we did have a chance.

"Jim is just over 30 seconds behind. Bit too much to make up, but he'll try anyway."

"Thanks Sarah, I'll give it a go" was my reply, though in the ever increasing noise levels, the sarcasm was lost on her.

"Go"

And off we went, bouncing off the little hummocks in the first few hundred meters of the race. Onto the hill and we were motoring. Again, down the long straight, really moving, and then reality set in. The tell-tale signs of both Maji and Fly just starting to hold back. It was just too fast for them. Nothing for it, apply the brakes and slow the team, not a lot, just enough to give the two of them a little breather. But, my race was over, I knew that now. To beat the guy ahead we needed to go faster than yesterday, and that was just not going to happen. But I was not going to give up my podium place. We could still keep our 2nd place, I just needed to be sensible. We made it down to the Loch, the dogs eased up and we settled and I started to relax. There was now no danger of over running the dogs, it was slightly up hill for most of the way now so I just let Joker and Dansa set their own pace. We cruised home; the dogs finishing strongly, and we kept 2nd. We were 36 seconds slower than yesterday but I was immensely proud of the dogs. Maji was positively ancient at over 10 years old, and Gun was still a baby. This would be Maji's last Aviemore, retirement loomed. Gun's career was just starting, things were looking good. We might have come 2nd, but we'd also beaten two previous 6 dog champions, and Joker had earlier won the Junior 1 dog race. We could hold our heads high.

Chapter 10

Reflections

Back home in Chichester I was now looking ahead to some more races. As Maji, Cougar and Bandit were starting to slow, I was wondering about formations for the following season when that was abruptly taken out of my hands.

The dogs, all being entire, used to have little niggles, but fortunately nothing serious. Just the odd cut here and there and only twice needing stitches, but they did tend to bite each other's legs. So would I if I was a dog, there is no chance of getting bitten yourself, legs do not have teeth. But they do have arteries near the surface.

I left for work on the Wednesday morning, having run the team the previous evening. They had worked really hard and I was now getting over my Aviemore disappointment. It was the 18th February. I came home that night, but something didn't feel right the moment I came up the drive. Normally the dogs greeted me with a rousing "chorus", which used to annoy the neighbours terribly. But they were only doing what a normal pack would do in the wild, greet the alpha male... Me. But they were all quiet, laying on their boxes, not even a tail wag from one of them.

"Ok boys, what have you done now?" I jokingly said to them.

I went into the nearest pen.

All seemed fine, Bandit still curled up in his box.

"Come on Bandy, good boy."

Nothing.

"Bloody hell Bandit, what's the matter, had a hard day lying in the sun have you?"

And I walked to his box to see him fast asleep.

"You lazy bugger," as I shook him, and I nearly collapsed.

He was stone cold and dead.

I was in a daze. I just couldn't understand this. He was fine when I left him that morning. Has he had a heart attack, a fit, what?

I picked him up in a daze and only then did I notice the blood. His blanket was covered in the stuff. But there was no major cut on him, and then I saw it. His right foreleg was red, and there just about half way down was the tell-tale mark. He'd been bitten and it had caught an Artery. He'd bled to death. There wasn't another mark on him.

In the pen were Maji, Raider and Gun. All males. There was also Fly, a female. And there was no telling who had bitten Bandit. I had my suspicions, but what can you do? You can't punish a dog without proof, and unless they suddenly developed the art of speech, I had to leave it.

I picked up Bandit and put him in the truck, and went inside and cried my eyes out. My beautiful Bandit, the friendliest dog I have ever owned was now lying dead in my truck. Never once in his life had he so much as bared his teeth at another dog. He was just so placid. Totally loopy yes, but aggressive, no. And just 10 years old. No age at all.

Pulling myself together I prepared the evening meal for the remaining dogs. I seem to remember that none of them were particularly hungry, but I can't be too sure.

Cherry luckily was at her brother's for a few days and it took me over a half bottle of my Malt whiskey before I plucked up the courage to phone her with the bad news.

She immediately burst into tears, and I had to recall the events of his death step by step. Eventually, both of us in tears, I had to put the phone down, and I literally drowned my sorrows.

I emptied the bottle.

Although, I took the dogs out after this disaster, it just wasn't the same without Bandit, and I had to force myself to at least attend a race meeting. I couldn't handle a big team so I decided to enter a 3 dog race, one day only, ostensibly to give Gun a bit more experience. I chose a meeting at Thetford and we won that day, Gun leading with Joker and Dansa at wheel, but I really did not enjoy that meeting.

Banter has always been a big part of dog racing, people are always taking the piss, and mostly it is taken for what it is, a bit of fun.

So to see me running a 3 dog so soon after running 6 at Aviemore was a God given opportunity, which was seized on by my competitors.

"How the mighty have fallen, the great Jim Bryde reduced to running a 3." A female friend.

Instead of just letting it pass, I reacted, and rather badly.

I let off a rant about "yea great fun isn't it, only running 3 because you'd cremated your leader who'd died two weeks ago. Yea, how the mighty have fallen!" and then I stormed off with tears welling up in my eyes.

I did catch up with her later to apologise, which was accepted, but never has the phrase "foot in mouth" been more apt.

Still, I got through it, and two weeks later, made a bit more of an effort, after all Gun was a youngster raring to go, and even if I didn't feel like running, he did. So we entered the Wellington rally, a favourite of mine. This is only about 2 miles long and is usually held towards the end of the season, basically because it's very tricky to get round. It's centred around a lake in a country park and the last mile is through and around a caravan park. All twists and turns where you need a very good command leader and "good brakes" For this reason I never ran a 4 dog there, the possibility of crashing being very high. I entered 3 adult teams, and a junior 1 dog to be run by Hughie's grandson Carl. He won, I had 3 second places, and that was the end of the racing season, Gun having entered 3 races, winning 2 and coming 2nd in the other, not bad at all.

Chapter 11

Fame at Last... I Think Not

With the racing season now over the pressure was off and we could have a bit of fun and experimentation.

Ever since I started racing, I reasoned that to rely on just one leader as most people did, would be a mistake, so all my dogs were trained to lead, bar none.

Made sense really, you could never tell when a dog would become injured, pregnant, get old and decide not to run any more, or just that they didn't fancy running that particular day. Not much different to humans really.

Consequently, even though I had my rock solid leaders in Joker and Dansa, they very rarely got to lead together on training runs. This was something that I also learned from Harris Dunlop's training manuals. He devised a routine that each dog would be rotated in the team, so one day they could be running right lead, next left wheel. If this was good enough for a former World Sprint Champion, and breeder of the Zero stain of dogs, who was I to argue? Joker, bless him, hated this, as he thought his place was leader, and quite often made his feelings known. Trying to get him into the team when he knew he wasn't going to lead could often be a nightmare. I had to pick him up as he refused point blank to walk to the gang line, and then once hooked up would sulk by dragging his feet until the natural enthusiasm of sled dogs took over, and then he would run his heart out.

Eventually though, I did relent and put him up front all the time. He was so fast that he was catching the dogs up ahead of him on most runs, and it was ruining training. The little tyke had lived up to his name "Joker", and didn't he wallow in his victory. So from the age of 5, Joker had his own routine to follow. Once we arrived at the training ground, I'd open the passenger door, he'd jump out, wander around while I parked up and unloaded the van and then stood patiently in lead position till I hooked him up first, and then he'd give his little "howl" of victory and a little smirk and wait till the rest of the team was put on and then take us all on a merry go round of a run. He enjoyed his work like no other dog I have ever known, my "one in a million"

Gun however was a different kettle of fish. I don't know where he learnt his party trick, although I'm sure Labbi had a hand. Gun was and still is a very friendly dog, likes everyone, never fights and is a joy to live with. But, trying to get him out of his cage could be problematic if you didn't know him.

Open the cage door to "Mr Friendly" and you would be greeted by a curled lip and a deep growl. Now even to a complete novice, this is the warning sign NOT to go too near, this dog was preparing to bite. Only he wasn't. You'd put your hand in the cage and he'd immediately lick it and quite happily jump out to be harnessed up. No problem at all. As long as you knew. I have to confess to sometimes asking unsuspecting but over cocky handlers to "Go and get Gun out for us, will you, he's the big black dog top right in the truck" and watch as they strode over to get him, and then back off alarmingly as Gun decided he was not moving and gave his "greeting", and then around to see me and my mates in the know roaring with laughter.

"Welcome to the world of real dog sledding" as one of us would then stroll over, get the same treatment from Gun, but knowing the truth, would get him out without a problem, and take him over to the "handler" for a proper greeting. Gun has carried this on all his life, but he's harmless. I think he missed his vocation in life, an actor. After all there was a film named after him; "Top Gun"

He was now starting to become a top class leader, just like his ageing dad Magi, and his mum Fly. I was starting to be very proud of him, but he was still 6th in line to lead but at least he wasn't last. That honour went to Raider. He should have been a world class lead dog. His father Cougar had lead my team many a time, and his mother was an amazing pure white bitch aptly named "Spooky" who was an amazing lead dog. His litter brother "Marin" became my mate Cathy's main leader for years. Raider was as they say "one sandwich short of a picnic". Very powerful, very fast, but just could not handle being leader. His first race ever was in 2 dog at Aviemore, where we finished up, you guessed it "2nd", Raider coming to the finish line paired with Labi, freaked out within 50metres of the finish. The noise of the crowds got the better of him and he just turned around and ran the other way. Luckily I had my wits about me, jumped off, and literally dragged him Labi and the rig across the finish line, and 2nd place. Never again did he lead. Wheel was his position, and he thrived there. And the lesson learned... You cannot guarantee a lead dog, no matter what anyone tells you and no matter the breeding.

Anyway, May 04 was now upon us and holiday season loomed, I had booked a week's hols in Turkey and decided to give the dogs one last training session. Hooked them up for a short 2 mile run, turned round to get on the quad, and in the corner of my eye saw Gun... running free up the trail.

Now for most Siberian Husky owners this would be a prelude to disaster, and the panic button would be pressed, followed by anxious screaming "loose dog".

You are constantly told by the "experts" a Siberian cannot be trusted off the lead. It will not respond to a recall, and it will just run and run until it either can't run anymore, or more worryingly, kill or be killed.

To a great extent this is true, a Siberian is not for the novice dog owner. It does have a very high prey instinct. **But** it can be trained to come back, after all it is a domestic dog, and domestic dogs can be trained to come back.

When I was a kid on the streets of Rock Ferry, I and all my mates had dogs, and not one lead between us. Our dogs just followed us everywhere, mine even used to wait outside my school gates for me to come out and walk the half mile back home together. To this day I have never been able to get a dog to walk alongside me on a lead, hence my aversion to show rings, I'm just bloody hopeless. But I can get a dog to come back to its name and walk alongside me off lead. And that's how I have treated every Sibe I have ever owned, as a domestic dog, albeit a bit of a handful at times.

Hustler was trained to the recall and Gun was as well, so I was not in the slightest bit worried.

Mounted the quad and called him, now about 100mts ahead. He didn't come back though, he did what Joker always used to do when he managed to escape... he sat down in the middle of the trail and waited till we caught him up.

Once alongside him, I stopped the quad, he went to the empty space in the gang line, next to his mum Fly, I hooked him up, and we carried on as though nothing extraordinary had happened. And in my mind nothing had, a dog had got off and I got him back straight away, no big deal. Training in the woods at night on your own and miles from civilisation you have got to be sure of your dogs. Anything can happen, a broken tug line, slipped collar, anything, and if you can't trust your dogs to come back to the recall, one bit of advice... don't go on your own, disaster is awaiting you.

Turkey came and went, training was spasmodic, it being that rare occurrence in England, a hot summer, when catching a few rays in the garden Cherry said there was someone on the phone from a film company. Fame at last, I thought, must have heard about me and the "Tomb Raider" filming I was involved with a few years ago.

The company was "Two Hand Productions" and wanted to know if I was interested in "doing a bit of filming with your Huskies up at Dunsfold airfield, near Guildford this Friday?"

"And what exactly would I be doing?"

"We'd like you and 4 dogs to race a caravan towed by an old car round a small oval track. Could you do that?"

"Course I can, what time do you want us?"

"Be here for 8am, do you know where we are?"

"Yea no problem, I work out of Whitley just down the road."

"Right see you Friday then."

I was over the moon. Dunsfold Airfield is the venue for the TV series "Top Gear". I was going to be on prime time Tele racing Clarkson. Let him try his smart-alec one liners on me. I'll show him.

Obviously I needed some handlers and Cherry as usual was just not interested. Can't really blame her, years of trailing around the country with me and the dogs had taken the shine off what was originally an exciting adventure. And to try and persuade her to like cars and caravans and muddy fields, well, that was one step too far. She declined gracefully.

Never mind, I knew who would do it, Hughie and his Grandson, the now grown up, Carl.

Friday, the 10th September 2004, saw the three of us arrive at the entrance to the airfield, all excited about the coming day's filming.

Carl was, and still is, a nut about cars and he was hoping he'd get a go alongside "The Stig".

"Carl, we're racing a rig and 4 dogs against an old banger and a caravan. I don't think the Stig's even going to be here," I heard Hughie say.

"But he might be, and I might even get a go in that Ferrari over there"

And right in front of us was a big fat bloke standing in front of the car, his back to us.

"Clarkson," we all chorused.

And then he turned round.

"That's not him, that's just a fat guy with a Ferrari, where's the Stig?" Carl was heard to say despondently.

"Hey Jim, notice anything odd?" Hughie asked.

"No not really, just a bunch of young lads gathered round that camera," I replied.

"Yea, lads, but no girls."

"So?"

And then the penny dropped for Carl. "You know, this is the place where they film that kids' programme 'No Girls Allowed'."

Hughie and I just looked at each other. You might just as well have said "Life on Mars is filmed here" We had no idea what he was talking about. We did though when the only female present wandered over, introduced herself (Forgotten her name) and explained what she wanted from us. This was a programme exclusively for teenage lads, no girls, and they set up events for them, boys' events.

In front of where we had parked was a small oval track marked out on the grass, about 200mts tops. I was to take the inside track, and try and get around and across the finish line before the stunt driver and his souped up old banger towing an old caravan.

Didn't seem to be much of a problem here, the dogs were used to racing near and alongside cars, so I decided to give it a go, doing a couple of trial runs before the real race the next day.

Hooked up 4 dogs, Joker and Gun in lead, and took off around the track, followed by a deliberately over revved banger towing an even worse looking caravan.

The dogs did not like this at all especially young Gun, and they put on the "turbo Charges" to get away from the noise.

And that's when it all went wrong.

The track was on a field that had been used for towing heavy machinery into position, and had left deep ruts. These are no problem as long as you run parallel to them, no problem at all. The problem comes when you try to turn, and at the speed we were going, it proved impossible.

I tied to "lift" the front wheel out of the rut, "asking" the dogs to slow down. Not a hope in hell, they just wanted to run and the inevitable happened, the front wheel jammed in the tracks.

And then I flew!

And then I landed, flat on my back, with the rig, which I had a death grip on, landing on my chest.

Didn't have a moment to think as I was catapulted forward and landed back onto the footplates of the rig, and carried on to cross the finishing line as though nothing had happened.

This was greeted by thunderous applause by the watching extras, who all assumed I'd done it on purpose.

Apparently, I had performed a perfect 360 degree somersault, landing on my back, and the speed and power of the dogs had dragged me back upright so fluently that it looked like a professional stunt. My badly bruised back said otherwise, and once I'd put the dogs away, the pain started and I feared the worst for the next day's filming.

But, on the bright side, Jeremy Beadles of "You've been framed" was just about to get a superb "stunt", and me a small fortune.

"Sorry lad, we weren't running the cameras... too expensive."

"Tell me you got that on your mobile Carl?"

"Sorry, never thought to film it."

"So no one got that on film?"

"No."

So there it was, my one chance of TV fame dashed.

And I didn't even get to appear on the show either.

The next morning I couldn't even get out of bed, I was in agony.

But the show must go on as they say, and when Hughie and Carl called round, with their help I managed to get dressed, load up the dogs, and went for the final day's filming of the race. Carl was to be my stand in, and both he and I expected him to win.

And then the "reality" of live TV programmes hit home.

The stunt driver was a permanent fixture on the show, and <u>Always </u>won his challenges, and this race was not going to be any different. Because I'd beaten him easily yesterday, he was to be given a head start, about 15mts. I was too far away to hear Carl agree to this. All I heard was the interviewer ask him if he was going to win.

"No problem at all, we're going to slaughter the guy," Carl rather arrogantly replied. He knew how fast the dogs were and on a tight track, the 15mts shouldn't cause too much of a handicap.

But it did.

The race started, the Stunt driver revved up his banger and roared off, suddenly his clutch control much better, not sliding around anymore. He won by a country-mile, and finished by flipping the caravan by driving it up a ramp. And the crowd of young lads went wild, and the stunt driver got out of his car and "milked" the applause.

The show had got what it wanted... a win... and everyone went home happy.

Except us, and especially Carl who was fuming.

But that's show business.

The good guys always win, especially if he's the resident stunt driver.

Chapter 12

Decisions

Filming now forgotten, it was now time to start training for the rapidly approaching new racing season.

I had during the summer been running the dogs on my new sand buggy. This was a brilliant bit of kit, so low slung that you could go round corners at full speed without any fear of it tipping over, ideal for fast speed work.

But this was now September and time to build their muscles up again. To do this meant going slower and making the dogs "pull". The best way to achieve this was to use a heavy rig, and I had a brute of a one. Having worked in Berlin a few years earlier I had met up with some local mushers and saw how they trained their dogs with very heavy 4 wheeled rigs. These were not used for speed just long slow runs, and had the advantage of having the space for a seated passenger. Because it was so heavy, you needed a fair size team to make it move. Having bought one and brought it home I decided to try it out, and somewhat foolhardy decided that fourteen dogs plus a passenger would be an ideal test. Why fourteen? Neil, my mate was now lodging with us, having split with his girlfriend Tanya some months earlier. Neil had the fastest team in Britain and I had often trained with him and now he was living at my place, it seemed logical for us to train together more often. Between us we had 26 fast running dogs and 1 heavy rig. So, the idea was to put on Neil's slower twelve first, get that out of the way and then the real test, my 8 plus his record breaking 6.

Now I thought this was a good idea, and the first run where I was the driver and Neil the passenger worked well. We went round the 4 mile course quite easily, and if I have to say so myself, under control and handled like an expert.

Then we put the 14 on.

Selhurst Park does have some flat parts, notably the mile long straight that runs parallel to the road running west/east and giving great views of the coast and Chichester and Bognor. But that road is on the crest of the South Downs, and to get to the trail at the bottom, you have to go down a hill; in places a very steep hill. Now as this was my main training ground, I very rarely went down the steep hills, the route we'd taken with the 12 dogs earlier was relatively flat, the only real sticking point being the 180 degree hairpin bend we'd had to negotiate to get us round the small loop that took us back on the same trail we'd just travelled. Neil was to take this turn when he drove, which is why I'd gone first, logical really, I would show him the way. What could go wrong?

The gang line was now "singing". 14 dogs all screaming to get going.

"Neil, you know where to turn don't you."

"Yes just after we leave the car park area and after the telegraph pole."

In the ensuing noise I could swear later that I heard him say "before" the telegraph pole.

"Yes that's right," I heard myself say. "Come on then let's get going, it's getting dark. Good luck."

And with that he pulled the quick release snub line and we shot off... too fast.

"Neil any chance you could slow them down a bit, it's a bit scary sitting here."

The combined weight of him and me and the rig was just over 500lbs and the speedo was showing 22 mph.

"Neil this is too fast."

"The brakes are not slowing them too much, but we'll be ok, they'll soon get tired, and then we can both start enjoying the ride. I'm not enjoying the speed too much myself, I don't have a great deal of control. You sure this is a German rig, and not some copy by the Chinese?"

"Funny," I replied sarcastically. "You just concentrate on the driving and put your headlamp on, I can't see a thing here, it's got dark quick."

"Haven't brought it with me, but we'll soon be home, so no worries"

"Neil you've missed the f.....ing turning," as the telegraph pole loomed ever nearer.

"No I haven't, the telegraph pole is right ahead, then I do a haw (Left)"

"You take the haw before the pole, NOT after."

"I'll just take the next left then, it won't be a problem"

Famous last words!

"Haw" rang out into the night and his leader Becky obeyed instantly, and my heart sank.

Ahead of us was the steepest trail in the park, and Becky was now out of sight.

Instead of a clear open trail, Neil was taking us down a narrow tree and gorse bush lined trail, and it was pitch black. The dogs had disappeared, apart from the pure white wheel dog "Salty". He was all I could make out of our rapidly running 14 dog team

"Shiiiiiiiiiiiiit" (Well that's the sanitised version of what we collectively screamed out.)

And we flew down that trail, bouncing off the spiky gorse bushes, hitting ever bump and ditch, and desperately hoping the ride would end. But I knew this trail, having ridden it once before, and I knew if we could make it to the bottom in one piece, it swung gently to the left and then gradually downhill till we hit the bottom car park before turning sharply left to go back to the top of the hill we'd just come down.

We made it... just. And in one piece.

"That was great, fancy another go tomorrow?" I heard Neil say.

"You're bloody nuts. Next time, if ever, you get to go as passenger, and then tell me if it's great."

This all came back to me as I got the rig out of the garage for its first run of the season. I was now down to 7 dogs, and the brothers Magi and Cougar were shortly to pass their 11th birthday, both slowing down now with age so this method of training was ideal for both of them. Couple of weeks on the heavy rig and I decided to give them a fast run on the sand buggy.

Normally after a few weeks of heavy training, the dogs ran like the wind on the buggy. This time though, both Cougar and Magi, held back; just could not cope with the speed. At their age this would not normally worry me, but Magi was also off his food, which did. He had always hungrily devoured his food, so to not eat properly was starting to worry me a bit. I would give it a couple of days and then if nothing improved take him to the vets. And then the bombshell.

I'd run them all Sunday afternoon, on the slower heavier rig, fed and watered them and put them all to bed, and went in to watch tele as usual, before the start of the weekly grind of going to work the next day.

Got up Monday morning, got the snacks for the dogs ready and went as usual to the kennels.

And Magi was nowhere to be seen.

Went to his box and he was still sleeping. But he wasn't... he was dead.

An almighty déjà vu hit me at this point, and I picked him up as I had done with Bandit 8 months earlier. But there was not a mark on him; not one. I couldn't believe it, my beloved Alpha male, my first true running sled dog, my Joe DiMaggio, had gone. (With apologies to Simon and Garfunkel's famous song Mrs Robinson) With tears flowing freely I picked him up, put him in the truck, told Cherry what had happened, and made the same journey I'd taken with Bandit those months earlier in the year. He was cremated the next day, and the sadness has never left either of us. I never did find out what he died of, just couldn't bring myself to have an autopsy done. He was dead, and nothing would bring him back.

I was now down to 6 dogs, and although we trained well and won the opening races we entered, my enthusiasm was elsewhere, and when a mate, Graham, asked if he could borrow my lead dog Joker for a couple of races, I jumped at the chance. It turned out that he needed a good strong lead dog for an 8 dog race he was entering in Scotland, a version of the British Championships that had surfaced over the past couple of years. None of these versions was ratified by any governing body, so I very rarely entered, but I had no objections to anybody else entering, after all it's a free world.

Joker was to be running lead with a dog I nearly bought a few years earlier, Chalkie. A very good lead dog, roughly the same age and size as Joker, so should be a good pairing. When I met Graham in Salisbury to hand over Joker I gave him the usual spiel about what he ate, sleeping arrangements (which Joker later decided for himself) and a warning not to put him up front straightaway.

"Let him find his way in the team first, then put him left lead."

Taking my advice he put him at swing (Just behind leaders) and running his usual training trail called out "haw" as they came up to the turn, expecting a smooth passage as usual.

Joker, had other ideas.

Just before this main turning was a small almost indistinguishable trail, you'd hardly notice it travelling at 20mph as Graham was doing.

But Joker saw it.

I had warned Graham that if you gave Joker a command, he would take it instantly. You could not give him a turn command 20mts ahead, it needed to be at the turning, or wherever you wanted to turn. All Joker knew was "Haw" meant go left... immediately.

Now this is brilliant if you want to be guaranteed of a turn, but you'd better be sure it's where you want to turn, or suffer the consequences.

Graham suffered!

Joker saw the "trail", and took it, dragging the front half of the team with him, and the remaining 4 dogs had no option but to follow. Luckily Graham had his wits about him, rode the turn and managed to stop and turn them around before he became injured. The "trail" becoming very twisty and dangerous a bit further along.

The next day Joker led... lesson learned.

Graham also found out that Joker liked females, and would do anything to be near them.

And he did not like being caged.

When riding with me he sat in the passenger seat, head hanging out the window, quite happy and contented. He would stay there all day, only getting out to go to the toilet or me getting him out to race. You could, and I often did by mistake, leave the door open and he would not budge. I remember going to the pub once and coming out after a couple of hours, noticed I had left the driver's door open, and fearing the worst, looked inside and there was Joker, snoring happily away waiting for me to return... an amazing dog.

I had warned Graham of this behaviour, but he either didn't listen or didn't believe me, and caged Joker in the kitchen, with his three bitches sleeping the other side of the central peninsula. Out of sight out of mind he thought.

He came down the next morning to find Joker and his three girls all cuddled up together. The cage, destroyed.

He wasn't caged again.

The 8 dog race didn't go as planned either. First day they were leading, but the second day a slip by Chalkie, and they lost by seconds.

The following week they redeemed themselves in a six dog race, with a blindingly fast time and first place. And that was it, Joker was returned, but not before disgracing himself by mating the bitch next to him on the stake out line as his own particular bonus for winning.

By now the total grief of Maji's passing was receding and my thoughts started to turn to Aviemore, this being the beginning of December.

With 6 dogs left I had no problems about who to leave out, they would all race. My problem would be who to run next to whom.

Fate, again took the decision out of my hands.

Gun was now 2 years old and getting into his prime. On 22nd December, his birthday, we celebrated his birthday with a brilliant fast run and his reward, a Tesco special, half a roast Chicken. If you can't spoil your dogs on their birthdays when can you?

So there I am dreaming of an Aviemore 6 dog victory, we really were motoring in training, when Boxing Day brought me down to earth with a bang.

We were going along at a very fast pace when about 1 mile from home, Cougar put his "feet down" and refused to run. The pace was just too fast for him, so as we were near the truck, I unhooked him from the team, and ran the remaining 5 back to the finish with Cougar running free behind us.

"Happy Retirement Cougar," I said as he jumped into the truck, "just slow training runs from now on, no fast sessions". And as he gave me a "howl" I believe he understood.

So within 10 months, I'd lost the nucleus of my team, Maji and Bandit gone and Cougar retired. Not a year to remember by any means.

"Never mind, next year will be better," I said to myself.

And as it turned out 2004 was a piece of cake compared to what was about to hit me in 2005.

Photos

Fly with her puppies, Pepper, Gun and Detroit.

Baggins Potter and Hustler. They would sit on the windowsill like this all day, to the astonishment of passers-by.

Hustler the 1st day I brought him home exhausted. My very first Siberian, the start of a long journey culminating at Aviemore 2011.

Powys Mid Wales and I have borrowed a rig ,lines and with Hustler have my first "go" at rig racing, courtesy of The SHCGB organising a teach in in 1989.

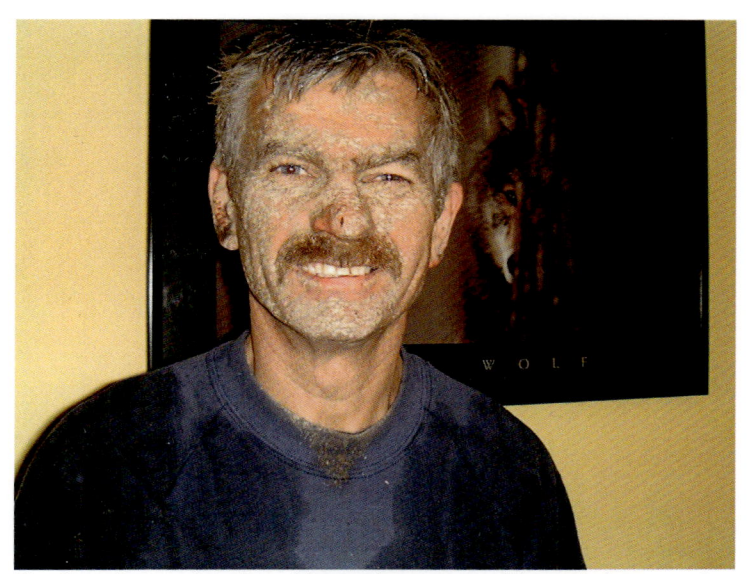

The first of many days I would come home covered in mud, thrown up by the dogs' feet and rig wheels. You never get this racing on snow.

Cassie, my beautiful and only couch potato Siberian. A wonderful girl who hated training and anything to do with racing.

In the French Alps during The trophie de Savoie, January 2003. L/R me, Arno, Fred, Shane, John, Keith and Dougie (now sadly deceased) Note the hi- tec sleds.

Us starting the 2nd day of the race at St Gervais. The 1st day we went UP the slope in the background.

What goes up comes down, the terrifyingly steep slope that singled the end of the race. Luckily I made it in one piece.

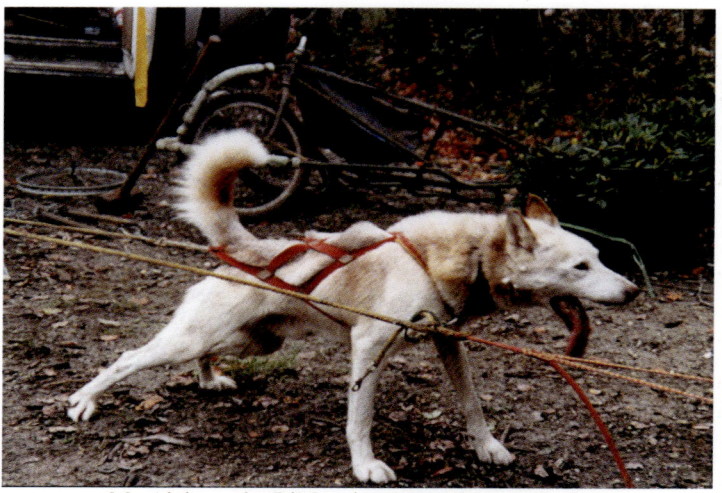

My Alpha male, DiMaggio, a powerhouse of a dog.

Bandit, the best looking dog I have ever owned.

Bandit was a lunatic, and here he has just decided to jump up into my arms, all 55lbs of him. Nuts!

Cougar in the car park in Aviemore. I have never seen a more graceful dog as him, he truly did move like a cougar, effortlessly.

L/R Cougar, DiMaggio, Joker at 6 months, Bandit and Labbi, in their pen at Brook Cottage, Chichester.

The Jokerman, my dog in a million, Joker.

Dansa even when he went blind, he still liked to run.

Raider, handsome but deadly!

Me winning 6 dog, New Forest, November 1999. All the dogs running in perfect symmetry at 19mph, Joker and Dansa leading, Dog running doesn't get much better.

Fly, looking worried in the front of the truck. She was on the way to the vets, whom she detested.

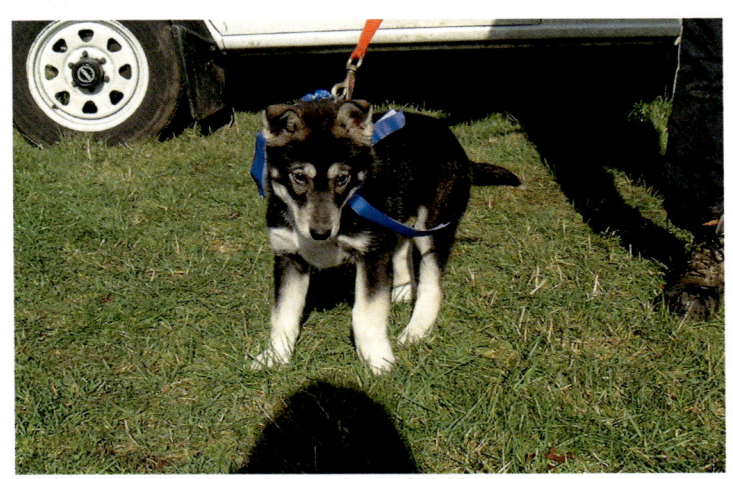

Gun at 3 months old.

A momentous occasion, Gun's very first run on a rig, next to the ever faithful 13 year old Labbi, with Ewan steering and me trying vainly to keep up with a clearly excited Gun.

Gun in show ring with Paul Keen.

Richmond Championship Dog Show
ASCOT RACECOURSE
September 5th, 6th & 7th 2003

RESERVE

JUDGE: PENNY EVANS
BREED: SIBERIAN HUSKY
CLASS No. 1090
EXHIBIT No. GUN

4th place certificate. We were robbed and never again would Gun be shown.

Gun's first race, 6 dog at Aviemore 2004. Both him and Dansa wore boots due to the abrasive surface. We came 2nd.

Gun relaxing at home at 14 months old with his mum Fly in the background.

Fly, Gun and Angel winning 3 dog at Wellington.

Joker in his truck with the damage he caused trying and succeeding in getting to Angel to mate her. The wood is half inch marine ply.

Reef and her amazing markings.

Naming pups is easy when they look like this. L/R Hobo, "teddy" Bear, Reef, Panda.

The pups at 6 weeks old. L/R: Panda, Reef, Jester, Hobo, and Bear. A very good looking bunch even if I say so myself.

At 6 months old Bear (in lead) next to Dansa with Reef and Angel at wheel (rear)

China my Bengal meeting Brew the Alsatian for the first time.

Brew makes a quick exit. China still attacks any strange dog, Huskies beware!

December 8 and Angel and Django enjoy free running in the snow, Chichester.

Fly, Dansa, Django, Angel enjoying the snow December 2008.

Reef. I had just got back from Scotland with her and made the mistake of taking her indoors. China the Bengal attacked her, she ran yelping upstairs and jumped out of the dormer window to escape. She landed on the Quad and that's where she stayed, out of harm's way of our cat. It's true Cats and Huskies don't mix!

December at Manor nurseries, Gun bringing in Father Xmas.

Joker being harnessed up, nice and easy as it should be.

My truck with Bear, Gun and Hobo.

Steve Hopley running Hobo, Bear and Gun (just behind Bear) at the World Championships 2008

The Cairngorms, Aviemore.

Gun looking forlorn after being rested for the 2nd day after being injured first day. I'm harnessing up Bear.

Bear, looking supremely fit, before going on to win 8 dog, 2009

Filming with Helen Skelton Aviemore, 2009. Dansa and Angel led her to victory.

Helen being interviewed after winning.

Bear and Reef after a training run. Lovely picture, and not the least bit tired.

Bear

Angel. After all the dogs had been run Angel would come over for treats from her mate Hughie (you can just see his finger). By this point she had been off the lead for about 1 hour and never once did she run off. And Huskies can't be trusted off lead!

Goodwood, January, 2010 Gun, Django and Angel, training in the snow whilst Django's damaged leg heals.

January 2010. Having persuaded a passing snow plough to "piste" the Main Road to Goodwood race course, I took advantage and ran Dansa, Fly and Angel on the prepared surface. Dansa is by now 12 years old and totally blind. An amazing dog.

Fly and Gun leading an 11 dog team in training, June 2010. The power of Fly is there for all to see. Within days she was dead from complications during an operation for a twisted gut. She was only 10 years old. A very sad day.

Car Park, Aviemore.

Checking the ice at the beginning of the hill.

And we're off. The start of our winning run l/r Reef, Gun, Django, Bear.

Press cutting and billboard showing me with The 4 dog trophy. Mine at last!

Gun and me France 2014.

Using 1 finger to type, the beginning of the book.

Chapter 13

Aviemore 2005

22nd – 23rd January

With Cougar retired I was left with 5 dogs, only 4 of which could run in "C" class, which I had entered.

The dilemma was who to leave out. In training we were flying, running 4.4 miles, four times a week on the Goodwood trails. This was 400metres further than the Aviemore race distance, so they would not have a problem getting round.

All I needed was to work out the 4 who would actually race, get the balance right and I reckoned we would be unstoppable. And that's where the problems started.

Joker even though he would be in his 10th year was going in at left lead. This was a no brainer and even "blind Freddy" as the Aussies say would pick him. He was the dog of a life time, still tremendously fast and my best leader. He was in.

Gun at 2 years old was not yet mature enough to lead, but he was outstandingly fast and more importantly, was my most powerful dog. He was in at wheel.

That left Dansa, Fly and Raider.

Fly and Dansa where both very fast lead dogs, with Dansa being the stronger of the two. He'd also lead the 6 dog last year. He was in at right lead.

Raider was a very powerful dog, 6 months younger than Joker but older than both Fly (6) and Dansa (7). He also hated Joker so always had to run behind him, for the obvious reason, if in front he would turn around and attack. He had also had a bit of history with Dansa, scrapping with him on more than one occasion. But he would run with Fly.

Looking back now it would seem obvious to even a novice, "drop Raider". That's what I should have done, make the decision.

And I did... the wrong one...!

Thursday evening 20th January 05, saw me load up my racing rig and my 5 racing dogs, and say goodbye to Cherry who as ever was staying behind to look after Cougar, Labbi and Cassie, my 3 oldies. She wished me luck and told me to be careful and I started yet again the long and arduous 650mile overnight journey to The Highlands of Scotland and Aviemore.

I'd done this journey so often I could do it blindfolded. Leave Runcton, up Vinnetrow road, and onto the A27 at Chichester. From here it was down past Portsmouth, before joining the M3 north of Southampton, up the M3 to Winchester, and then road numbers galore. A34-M40-M42-M6, I'm getting tired even thinking about it, before hitting my first and only stopping point at the superb Lakeland service station, just south of Penrith.

Here the dogs are let out for a toilet break and a deserved "bark" at the resident water fowl on the ornamental pond (yes you heard right, a large duck pond at a service station in England). I then grab a well-deserved coffee and Guinness and Ale pie (This really is a service station) before climbing back in the truck to do the next 300 miles hoping to arrive around daybreak at the car-park next to the start line of the race, some miles outside Aviemore itself on the banks of Loch Morloch.

Typically I'd got my calculations wrong and arrived at 5am, still pitch black and sunrise a few hours off yet, so out came the sleeping bag to try and get a few hours well-earned sleep.

And it was now that Madame Fly finally, after 650 miles, lay down to go to sleep.

She was a notoriously bad passenger, and refused point blank to lay down in her travelling box like any normal "knackered" Husky. Because "knackered" she must be. But she always stood up when travelling, every time, and she always annoyed her travelling companions, as she constantly shifted her position, treading on them as she moved around trying to get comfortable. This often caused minor skirmishes, but was solved when she had Gun. He became by default her travelling companion. No one else would put up with her. Luckily Gun being her son had no choice in the matter. Fly was "boss" and he did as he was told.

Once the sun rose things started to warm up, and I decided to get up, shrugging off my hot water bottle "Joker" in the process. Whenever I camped in the truck he would sleep on top of me providing brilliant and very welcome heat. Every home should have one... and you don't even have to bother with boiling a kettle. "Superb" as we say in Merseyside.

Stepping outside it wasn't just the cold that hit me. It was the frozen white stuff I was standing on; ICE.

Joker and I gingerly made our way along the couple of hundred metres to the start of "the Hill" and my heart sank. We couldn't get up it. It was sheet ice. This was going to be a disaster. If the weather didn't improve, i.e. warm up, the race would be cancelled. It would be too dangerous to run dogs on that surface and to try and get them to pull a 3 wheeled rig would be suicidal. You would have no steering, brakes would be ineffectual, and whilst this would be fine going up the hill, assuming the dogs could get traction in the first place, going down the other side would be like watching "Bambi's" first venture onto the frozen lake. Legs everywhere. Not very appealing at 20 odd mile per hour. I decided to at least carry on and have a look at the rest of the trail, and was greatly relieved to see it was not as bad as the hill all the way round. Meeting one of the Forest rangers half way round, he said that a machine had been ordered to "Scrape" the ice off the hill, and by Saturday the trail would be fit to run.

Can't say I was totally convinced, but as a local he was, so I carried on till the end, still trying to figure out who to drop. The dogs had been running magnificently and I was totally confident of victory, no matter which four I finally chose.

Returning back at the car park and my starting point, I met up with my mate Sue, who was going to borrow whichever dog I "dropped" to run with her young Malamute. She was due to run in D2 class, meaning 2 dogs, one a husky and the other a Malamute. Problem was her Husky had been injured and she had phoned me up asking if I had a spare dog. She was over the moon when I said I had, but would have to wait till I came to Scotland to decide who she was going to have, her living in Aviemore itself.

Because of this situation, we had no choice but to let her "Mal" do the picking. "Mals" especially big males can be very aggressive to other dogs, the ultimate "alpha male". And at roughly 120lbs of muscle and bone with an impressive set of teeth to match, they were not a breed for the novice owner. Sue had owned Mals for years and regularly used to train with me when she lived down south, so I wasn't particularly worried about the temperament of this new dog.

Pulled "Raider" out first and her Mal upon seeing him let out the deep warning growl that we both knew well.

"Looks like he doesn't like him, let's try Dansa next"

Same outcome, deep warning growl and Dansa put smartly back in his box.

"Well, let's hope he likes ladies 'cos Fly is all I have left"

Out came Fly, who dragged us over to the Mal, immediately took a shine to this "big boy"; turned her back on him and offered her backside to her new "beau".

"Such a slut... she'll do fine" said Sue as she realised she at least now had a team to run.

That left me with my two preferred leaders Joker and Dansa, with the two powerhouses at wheel, Gun and Raider. They would certainly run well as a team; both pairs were matched in height and weight, and to an outsider they would look like the perfectly matched team. But... and the doubt was there from the start, I had a niggling feeling that this was not the right choice. However I had to drop one dog and at least Fly would get a run instead of sitting out the weekend in the back of the truck, sulking.

Thinking no more about it I headed off to book in at my B and B, a very nice and warm stone cottage just a stone's throw from The Coylumbridge Hotel, where the "Mushers' Meeting" was to take place at 5pm that evening.

Aviemore is the one race in the British Race Calendar where all mushers are required to attend a race briefing the night before the race. At every other race the meeting is held usually near the start chute of the race, and about 1 hour before the start of the race itself. Start times for the competitors have already been drawn and posted for all to see on a makeshift billboard, usually the side of someone's truck, and the meeting just points out the trail route and any difficulties you may encounter on the way round. Thus you have a stage for the budding "John Bishop's" out there who come up with gems like "then you come to a small rise in the trail" when in fact it's a 3:1 monster of a hill. All of this is taken in the mushers' stride, with banter flowing freely until the first race starts when the mood changes, and the competitor in us all appears.

The Mushers' meeting at Aviemore is quite different though, and is widely anticipated, by most of the blokes anyway as the first item on the agenda is "Whisky Tasting".

And not just any old Whisky... It's Single Malt.

And there are about 150 to choose from... all free.

Now this could be a disaster waiting to happen or a heaven given Godsend, depending on your point of view, for those like me who happen to like a drop of Scotland's best export... bar none. If you can see the fault in this (and visions of all the male mushers getting paralytic for free), well so did the S.H.C.G.B when this idea was first mooted.

So a solution needed to be found before the stampede to the bar.

As you come into the hall, you have to sign in, get your ceremonial sponsored sweat shirt, your miniature bottle of whisky, hand back any trophies you'd won the previous year and are given 3 raffle tickets.

One raffle ticket equals one free shot of Malt.

And that's why old standing club members of the SHCGB are so very knowledgeable about Malt, every Aviemore they get to practice free. Once all that has been downed – it's on to the serious business, the draw.

This is widely anticipated, everyone beforehand having decided who the favourites for each race will be, and greet their number being called with either catcalls "you're rubbish" or thunderous clapping "there's the winner". Everyone has an opinion, me included and they make sure it's heard.

As I hadn't even started my racing campaign this season, preferring to let the Finnegan brothers Carl and Luke run the team, for once I was coming in under the radar. This suited me fine, and I left the inevitable party after the meeting, confident and happy.

I had some decent mushers off in front of me, none of the dreaded "rookies"(first timers) who bless them, sometimes let the occasion get to them and mess up on the trail by making overtaking nearly impossible.

Early dinner and bed for the dogs, "Fish Supper" for me and then off to bed, confidence oozing.

I was ready.

Arriving at the car park next morning, at what I thought was a reasonable time, 7am, I was amazed to find it almost full, some 200 vans already parked up and over 1000 dogs already howling with excitement.

I eventually found a place to park, the trail having been deemed fit to race after the slight thaw overnight.

I was off middle of some 50 runners, start time nearly three hours away, so I walked the dogs, had yet another cup of tea, and waited.

And that's the worst part.

I spend the hours up to the start in a continual state of nervous energy, and I'm forever asking "You haven't got the time have you?" to anybody that passes. And on my dashboard is a big clock, and next to it is a stop watch. I know the time, but it's just a way of getting the nerves out of the system. That and going to the toilet, again and again and again. And why wouldn't you, 3 cups of tea every hour will do the trick for anyone.

Fifteen minutes to go.

Nerves are on edge.

Ten minutes to go, your handlers turn up and you harness the dogs.

Get the leads down, give each of your helpers a dog and it's the long walk to the start line, from where I'm parked some 300mts. I have never been able to walk my own dogs to the start line, I'm much too hyper for that, and as the dogs would feed off this, I always use handlers. Now my boys, Joker, Dansa, Raider and Gun, were frantically dragging their handlers down to the start line. Only one instruction was given to them. Keep Raider away from Joker... period.

We arrived in the holding area, spotted my rig that I had parked up there 2 hours earlier, re-examined it again for the umpteenth time, and moved slowly down the line till we were within 20mts of the start chute. Here I took control of the team and hooked them up to the rig in their allotted place on the gang line.

Things were now starting to pick up pace.

Because of the number of entries in the Rally, (50 alone in my class) and to make sure everyone took off and was back in daylight, the time gaps between all teams from C class (4 dog) had been cut to a very short minute. This proved very popular with the watching crowds but did nothing to calm mushers' nerves, already shredded to near breaking point by now.

Because of these time constraints, what we were forced to use was the so called "Alaskan Start".

At every other rally on the circuit you had at least a two minute time gap to the team in front. This allowed you to get your rig, put it on the start line where two "snubbers" tied it to a quick release rope, thereby ensuring everyone started from the same place. Once secured you then put your dogs in place on the gang line, thank all your helpers, have a cup of tea (Ok that bit's made up) and wait for the off. The point is you had plenty of time. With the Alaskan start, your team were already hooked up to the rig and you relied on your handlers to keep tight hold of the dogs as they dragged you to the correct point on the line... and hopefully hold firm.

This works brilliantly on a sled, the snow hook easily able to stop your team... dead. It can however have disastrous consequences when your rig only weighs 15kgs soaking wet and about as much grip on your slick tyres as Bambi on ice. One slip by a handler can see the team surge ahead down the trail, and instant disqualification.

Luckily at Aviemore there is a small bridge to cross before the start chute which allows the handlers to prevent this happening, but it could.

So now it's what I've been waiting for; my turn to race.

I'm called up... 197, Jim Bryde 1 minute to go.

The handlers get dragged forward by my team, I am standing on the back of the rig, brakes fully locked and then the snubbers do their job, the rig is secured and we're safe, and ready to go.

Well at least I was.

"Thirty seconds to go Jim" Sarah calls out over the Tannoy system.

And my team at this point are stood stock still, not howling, just staring down the trail, as nonchalant as you like.

"Eh Jim, you sure those dogs of yours are up for this. They don't look interested. You sure they are going to run?" the snubber asks.

"What?" I reply.

"I said you sure you know what you're doing, those dogs of yours don't look up to it, it's 4 miles long this race." Obviously they had picked a "newbie" as a snubber. He didn't know me from Adam.

"I think so," I replied as innocently as I could. "It's just that they are waiting for the 10 second count."

"Yea right, counting dogs," was his sarcastic reply.

"Fifteen seconds to go."

"Hold really tight on the ten," I shouted down "Do not let go";

14 seconds to go.

"Really?" came the reply;

13 seconds to go.

"Really," I was starting to get a bit pissed off by now.

12 seconds to go.

"Counting dogs... phaw";

11 seconds to go.

"Hold tight."

"Ten seconds to go Jim." Sarah's dulcet voice over the Tannoy.

"Holy shit, what the hell's happened to those dogs" came the startled voice of the doubting snubber as his arm is nearly wrenched from his socket as the team in unison surge forward.

"Told you they could count, hold extra tight on the 5"

Joker and his equally lunatic son Dansa were now trying to rip the rig from the hands of the two snubbers, and I was doing my best to hold them back by leaning back on the rig with brakes fully locked. The noise at this point was deafening, the dogs leaping frantically in the air.

5 - 4- 3- 2- 1- GO!

And that was it, we shot off down the twisty first part of the trail, rig bouncing off the little hummocks lining it, praying that we make it to the start of the hill, where they would calm a bit, and also let me catch my breath.

We made the bottom of the hill and the dogs now dug in and started to work... pulling relentlessly and, more importantly, fast, so much so that we caught and overtook the team who had started a minute before us, before we even made the summit.

"You're flying boys."

"Hike on Joker."

"Good boy Gun."

And then we crested the hill.

My mind was racing now. We'd done the hard part, well the dogs had, and now it was time to really let them loose.

And we screamed down the trail, me grinning from ear to ear, crouched as low as possible on the rig, not just for aerodynamics, but to hide behind the rig bag to fend off the gravel that the dogs where kicking up with their feet. And as we were travelling well in excess of 25mph, it hurt when a bit of gravel smacked you in the face, the rig bag was a Godsend.

With Joker and Dansa leading, the team were in their element, running as they were born to do, and they were loving it. We were overtaking at will screaming out "trail" as slower teams moved out of our way on our relentless run down to the Loch, and the slower part of the course. And oh so soon we were there, the right hand turn along the scenic part of the trail along the banks of Loch Morlich.

This is where the race can so easily be lost.

If you have run your dogs too fast down the hill and they are not fully fit, this part of the course will find them out. The trail winds ever so slightly uphill, and with it being very sandy in parts, can become a very heavy drag on your wheels, slowing you to a stop if you are not careful.

The two wheel dogs Raider and Gun now proved their worth to the team. These two powerhouses took all this in their stride and we rode along at a fair old pace, overtaking a couple of struggling teams, me giving the team a helping "hand" by scooting and everything was going brilliantly , and then I saw the "little hill". This "monster" comes about 800mts from the finish, and although it's only about 50mts in length, and not that steep really, after the scooting and adrenaline rush you've had for the last 3 and a half miles, it's a killer. Well it is to an old fogey like me. Younger fitter mushers take it in their stride. Me I dreaded it, every time!

"Come on fellas, all the way home" I screamed at the dogs.

This is the command that tells them their work is nearly done, only about 500mts to go and they didn't fail me. The turbo burners that they possess when they hear this command kicks in, and with me helping them by scooting, even though the lactic acid was burning my legs, we hit the top, and I must confess a whoop of joy left my lips. We were home and dry.

You're now into a very, very fast and enjoyable last part of the course, for both you and your dogs. The finish is in sight, the dogs can see and hear the welcoming crowd and go even faster.

We screamed across the finish line with so much speed and power that even with the brakes fully locked it took us a good thirty metres to slide to a stop.

We were in the lead. We'd done what we'd set out to do.

I was ecstatic. The hard work had paid off. And the dogs were still fresh and full of running. Roll on Sunday!

My handlers had waited at the finish line for me and now after hearty congratulations, put leads on Joker and Dansa and proceeded to guide me back to my van. Me; my head was in the clouds. We'd been the only team to go under 15 minutes for the 4 mile course and I had about a 15 second buffer to take to the start line on Sunday. And I made a mistake. Your race is not over in one day, it's a two day race, and I had momentarily forgotten that fact. And it came back to bite me very, very hard. I just wasn't concentrating as the crowds got very dense as we made our way up the small hill leading to the car-park. My job on the rig was to keep the gang line tight as my two handlers guided us through the crowds. And I didn't watch as they suddenly had to stop. Joker and Dansa stopped too. Unfortunately, I didn't, and neither did Gun, and neither did Raider. He saw his chance, and in the blink of an eye, had enough slack to dart forward, sink his teeth into his hated enemy Joker, and my race ended there. Finished. I just could not believe my eyes. Joker's front leg erupted in a crimson flush as the blood poured out from the 4 puncture wounds inflicted by Raider's canine teeth.

My handlers quickly realised what had happened, unhooked Joker, as I drove the rest of the team back to the van. I had all the dogs watered and put away by the time Sue arrived back with a limping Joker.

"Doesn't look good Jim, his leg's swelling up already" as a stricken Joker hobbled towards me.

By now there was quite a crowd gathered around as first news of my lead spread around and then the incident that followed.

"How is Joker?", "Will you be able to run him tomorrow?", "Back luck Jim" were just a few of the comments I heard as the reality set in.

Without my lead dog I was out of the race.

I spent the rest of the day and that night, massaging and bathing that front leg in an effort to get Joker fit for Sunday's race. Huskies have remarkable powers of recuperation and what would put a normal dog out for weeks would be shrugged off as nothing more than a scratch by these wonderfully tough and resilient dogs. And Joker was one of the toughest.

After spending the night on the bed with me in my Band B, Joker was his normal self in the morning, bouncing around and giving me grief till I took him out for what he wanted, to go to the toilet.

He stood on all fours to do his "business" and a look at his leg explained why. The swelling had subsided a bit, but the wounds were still weeping, and I had no idea what to do.

I could drop him from the team, and run a three, Dansa was quite capable of running single lead, but we would lose. I could take the easy option and scratch (not start), but as the leader of the race, that would be unthinkable, "go out on your shield" as the saying goes. I didn't think it would be fair to ask another "musher" what to do so I did the only thing possible, I asked Joker.

And he said "Go for it"

He didn't really speak, he just went lunatic when I showed him his racing harness.

He wanted to run, and I was not going to deny him.

He would be 10 on July 5th, this would be his last Aviemore and after coming 2nd four times I owed it to him to give him his last hurrah.

He had been the outstanding dog of his generation, still to this day headed the fastest team and fastest average speed during a timed race, 21 mph , and he deserved one last go at Aviemore glory.

We lined up at the start, everyone wishing us well, all knowing I was running an injured dog, and soon we were off.

The race itself was a bit of a blur, all I remember was Joker valiantly trying to lead the team to victory. I could see he was nowhere near as fluid as normal, the second day for us usually being faster than day one.

We crossed the finish line with Joker carrying his leg, 17 seconds down on yesterday's time.

I didn't wait to see what the rest of the times were.

We only had a 15 second lead over the second placed team.

It wasn't enough and I knew it.

But it was close, ever so close.

Martin Owen, running 4th on Saturday crossed the line and won by 0.07 seconds.

7 hundredths of a second... a hair's breadth.

It was later rounded up to a second, but it didn't matter, we had lost by the smallest margin ever.

But I was proud of my team, and Joker got the biggest hug ever.

"Happy Retirement Champ, you're still the best."

Chapter 14

Mixed Emotions

I drove home that night after the presentations in a bit of a daze.

I had been so confident of finally winning at Aviemore that this failure really got to me, and it lasted for years.

I was determined not to let it affect my dogs though, and on the Tuesday took them all out for a run, where they all ran brilliantly, Joker leading the team without a care in the world, two days too late.

But I had my dogs... and I was happy.

And today was Saturday 29th January and they all were waiting for me to return from my shopping expedition in Chichester. As well as being able to count at the start of a race, they also had the ability to know the days of the week. And Saturdays at my Kennels was "bone day". I had a deal with the local butcher that Saturday morning I would come in and buy for the princely sum of £5 whatever he couldn't sell due to it being "out of date". So the dogs waited eagerly for me to return and give them the contents of the surprise package. Anything could be inside, in summer it was usually meat covered in BBQ sauce, but middle of winter this was never going to happen. I pulled out however some lovely lamb chops and chicken legs, and the dogs in unison "drooled".

Calling each dog by name, I lobbed the food into the pens, where it was caught and devoured, in the case of Gun, practically whole, he very rarely chewed anything. And never once was there any argument, they would all wait patiently knowing that there was plenty to go around. In fact more often than not, too much, and each dog had its own bit of pen it retreated to, to "bury" the surplus to be dug up later as a tasty dirt filled morsel. Lovely!

Cassie my 14 year old "couch potato", was by this time living totally in the back garden, flatly refusing to go back either into her pen, or come inside the house, it being "too warm", except when food was on offer. Then she would suffer the heat, panting, until she got what she came for, food, and then go back outside to sleep. A typical Siberian, what would be cold to us would be considered positively baking to them with their double coats.

I called her over and showed her a big piece of Chicken, whereupon she did her party piece of running around in circles until I put her out of her misery and gave her the meat.

And then something odd happened, she started to cough... abruptly. She was frantic, and I immediately thought she had something caught in her throat. I caught her and opened her mouth to see what the problem was and she collapsed, literally. She was barely breathing, and whilst Cherry comforted her, I was on the phone to the vet. I explained what had just happened and he said to bring her in immediately.

I rushed back outside and found her standing up as though nothing had happened, "what's all the fuss?" she seemed to be saying, as she carried on chewing the bone.

But knowing what had happened with her mate Hustler, I decided to be safe and take her to be examined.

Once there a quick examination, and a diagnosis that was not good. The vet explained that due to her age, the muscles in her throat affecting her breathing had deteriorated and when she became excited, they collapsed and she couldn't breathe. The solution was an operation to tie back these weakened muscles (flaps). At her advanced age this was never going to be an option, so the suggestion was painkillers and an injection to try and keep her calm.

Took her home and within the hour, Cassie was in difficulties again, choking. It's at times like these that, and I know it's a cliché, you have to do the right thing. I couldn't put her through the ordeal of an operation that might or might not work and I couldn't let her suffer choking.

I called the vet who put Cassie to sleep in my arms in her beloved back garden. She was now at peace.

The next day, Sunday, I'd arranged to go training with Hughie, and I was dreading telling him about Cassie, and I was debating whether to call the whole thing off, but amazingly, Cougar, who had given up running, astounded me by pushing his way out of the pen and jumping up into the dog truck... he wanted to go running. He hadn't trained since I had to drop him back in December, but dogs know their own mind, so off we went to catch up with Hughie at Goodwood.

Once there I told him about Cassie, and once over the shock, we set about training the dogs. Just to be on the safe side I "booted" Cougar. These are a great bit of kit, originally developed to protect dogs' paws from harmful ice particles, but have been adopted over here by mushers to protect dogs' pads from the harmful gravel/stony trails that we have to use.

Into the team Cougar went, and you'd never thought he'd been away. One month off and he ran as though he hadn't missed a day's training. These dogs never cease to amaze me, they just never give up. After giving him another run on the Tuesday, I thought, in for a penny in for a pound and entered him in the next rally, Pembury, South Wales.

This was one of the few rallies that ran a class for veteran dogs, 7 years and older.

Originally it was thought a dog reached his peak at 7 years, and it was all downhill after that. But advances in training and nutrition meant dogs could and still perform at a much older age, so these classes were as rare as snow at Aviemore. As Cougar was now 11 and a half I was going to take full advantage and enter him in C class. However one of the peculiarities of this class was that the average age of the dogs entered had to be over 7, meaning you could run a youngster with an oldie as long as they averaged 7 years old.

As I only had 2 dogs younger than 7; Fly at 5 and a half and Gun at 13 months, this was never going to be a problem for me, all I had to do was decide who was going in C class veteran and who was going in E (3) class. Originally I was going to run three oldies; Cougar, Joker and Young Dansa 7 in the veteran and Raider, Fly and Gun in 3 dog, and that was the plan until I arrived on site and two unrelated events changed my mind.

Entered into C class (veteran) was my mate Cathy. Cathy and I had started out all those years ago together, we had roughly the same dogs; she had Bandit's litter brother and also Raider's litter brother. She had dominated the 2/3 dog class for years, having very, very fast dogs and weighing 6 stone soaking wet if she was lucky, was practically unbeatable. As she would be running 4 dogs, there was no way my three would beat her. I had to think again.

Then another incident occurred which really riled me.

I walked over to the start line where the starting times for the day's racing were posted and the usual gaggle of mushers were gathered, the topic of conversation was who was going to win each class. Usually I never bothered voicing my opinion; I let my dogs do the talking for me. I'd just returned from Aviemore, where even though I had lost, I still posted the fastest 4 dog round of the weekend. Then I heard the comment, "See Gareth is here again, there's your 3 dog winner."

Now I'd been racing for years and I'd never heard this name before, never even laid eyes on him.

"So who's this Gareth guy then?"

"Gareth, he's got dogs from your mate Fred, and he's won every 3 dog race he's entered this season, 10 I think so far."

"Really?"

"Yea, and usually by 2 minutes plus. He's unbeatable."

"Really? If you look I'm entered in 3 dog."

"Yea, but he's fit and runs and you don't do 3, you do 4. No, he'll win."

"Tell you what, he won't beat me by 2 mins, in fact he won't even beat me!" and I walked off leaving them all, dumbfounded , and me wondering how I was going to live up to my boast and beat "Superman". To say I was pissed off would be putting it bluntly. If you had a top class 4 dog team, all you had to do was drop your weakest dog, enter the 3 dog and you would most probably win. Three dog was an in between class, you had too many dogs for 2 dog and not enough to enter C class (4).

So who to run. Joker's leg had mended since Aviemore, and he was running at his best again. As a youngster, he had run against Cathy's unbeatable 2 dog team and won, much to her disgust and surprise. And when run in 3 dog he was virtually unbeatable. Even at 10 years old he was still awesome. Forget the veteran class, he would lead 3 dog. Up front he would be partnered by his daughter Fly, the dog Fred had given away. She was as fast as Joker, one of the few dogs that was. And bringing up the rear was my secret weapon, Gun, my powerhouse of a wheel dog.

And nobody had the slightest inkling of what was to come.

As fate would have it, Fred was out 2 mins in front of us, and he never gave us a second glance. Off he went and then it was our turn.

Fly, obviously peeved at missing out at Aviemore, was out of the starting chute like the proverbial bat out of hell.

We flew round the course, and nearing the end saw the familiar crouching style of Fred frantically scooting his rig, trying to get to the finish line before us.

Now in the tight knit community of dog racing, you do not want the indignity of being overtaken, and certainly not by your mate, and him running a bitch that you'd given away, and to rub salt into the wound, her yearling son, Gun. No the piss taking after would be unbearable, and he knew it, and he was trying desperately for this situation not to happen.

Me, I was loving this as Kevin Keegan once famously said, and seeing Fred I called up "all the way home" and the turbo that I was riding burst into life. The difference in speed was astonishing, Fly stuck her head down and exploded forward, Joker and Gun followed suit and it was like riding a 911, we flew.

I had no doubt that within 50mts we would call trail on Fred, overtake him and make him eat dirt as he watched my disappearing backside storm down the trail.

Here we go, this will be sweet, and then my heart sank. Fred had just passed the yellow "No ROW" sign, and with the trail narrowing dramatically, my chance had gone.

In sled dog racing, you are doing a time trial, just like bike riding, so overtaking is relatively rare, given that the starting positions are mostly manipulated by the organisers. Most races are run on fairly narrow trails, and trying to overtake using a fairly wide rig, could and usually does lead to problems, not least, dogs from both teams fighting each other as they come together.

Organisers have solved this by the simple solution, of insisting that the team being overtaken gives way, a la Formula one.

As soon as you get within a couple of teams' length of the team in front — you call out "trail" and as long as you have an experienced musher in front of you, they will pull over, sometimes even stop, to let you pass uninterrupted. But there was one exception to this rule.

The "No RoW" zone. No Right Of Way. This comes into effect in the last 800mts of the race, and here the rules do not apply. For the very simple reason, the end of the race is in sight – usually the trail is wide enough to overtake, and after all nobody in their right mind is going to stop and let someone pass within sight of the finish. And Fred was in the Zone. He knew the rules, and he was not going to let me pass – ever.

He slowed his scooting, and I swear he glanced over his shoulder, grinned at me, and slowly made his way to the finish line. He and his team had given their all to get to this point, and he was not about to throw it all away so near to the line. Gritting my teeth, I crawled in as well, putting the brakes on and getting quizzical glances from my team. Finally though the trail widened in the last 100mts and I called up the team and we passed Fred before the finish, satisfied with my morning's work.

Now it was back to the truck, water the team, put them away and prepare for the C class veterans in an hour's time. We had no hope of winning this, it was my 3 oldies against Cathy's 4. Still we would give it a go, and came home in 2nd place... to Cathy. Again watered the team, put them in the truck and strolled over to see my 3 dog time. Up in 1st place was, surprise, surprise; Fred's protégé Gareth. But only by 4 seconds. But this was a two day race, you got nothing for being first on day one, except the privilege of going out first on day two. Still, there were a lot of smug faces at that time sheet, all giving knowing glances saying "told you so, Gareth is leading again"

Sunday and I'm at the start watching Gareth take off. To be fair he goes off at a cracking pace, no doubt dreaming of a further victory for his young team. Then I parked my lot on the line, and Fred who'd been handling for Gareth, now took a look at my team. Having used Joker for mating purposes, he knew him well. What he didn't know was the dog up front and the big powerhouse at wheel.

"Who are the other two dogs then? Haven't seen them before."

"The dog at lead is Fly, the bitch you gave me, and that's her son Gun at wheel."

And Fred's face was a picture.

5-4-3-2-1-Go.

We screamed around the course, the team revelling in the ideal conditions the course presented; grassy, hilly, twisting, just as they liked it.

We came in 20 seconds faster than day one, and won by a total of 30 seconds.

The protégé had been dethroned.

In C class we consolidated our position, coming in a very good second.

Gun had performed brilliantly in his debut season, Joker was going out as a winner, and Fly was back to her very best, Cougar in the vet team had run without any problems. All was well in team Leahrno.

There was one race left in the calendar, a new venue down at Frilsham Forest near Eastbourne. I'd promised the organisers, who were 1st time organisers that I would help out and bring my Quad for trail marshal duties, and to enter at least 2 teams, thereby helping to get a decent entry quota.

As Cougar was back running, he was to be paired up front with his mate Dansa, with Fly and Raider at wheel. As this was only a one day rally, I reckoned he would be fine, and so it proved, they came 2nd over what was a very stony course, and Cougar excelled. I of course was made up, I had my dog back.

But the real bonus was to come later that day.

Gun had never run lead in competition yet, but today was his chance.

He was going to be paired with Grandad Joker, and I was really looking forward to it. This would tell me if Gun really was the real deal. Bring it on!

And didn't he just!

He and the "old man" absolutely destroyed the rest of the teams, flying round the course at a tremendous speed, winning by the almost unbelievable margin of 6 minutes.

I had found Joker's successor.

The king is dead, long live the King... Gun.

And it got even better.

Arriving home, I received a rather strange phone call from a mate who'd previously borrowed Joker, and now had another request.

Graham Good had at this time arguably the fastest 6 dog in Britain, he'd already won Aviemore and now he wanted to borrow Gun to improve his team.

"I've entered a race for "The British Championships" 5/6th March at the Forest of Ay, Scotland. It's very hilly and I need more power in my team. Saw what you did at Aviemore, should have won, but I would like to win this race. Any chance I could borrow your wheel dog, Gun isn't it?"

Now this was praise indeed.

The top rated musher in Britain wanted to borrow my yearling dog to improve his chances of winning a top race. Well I didn't need to think about it. It was the end of the season for us, Graham had previously borrowed Joker and returned him safely, so the answer was "Yes". We agreed to meet at Salisbury the next day, same dropping off place as before.

Gun, being a young dog, had not developed any idiosyncrasies yet (they would come later), so there was no big list of "Does and Don'ts like with Joker.

Upon meeting Graham, I introduced him, and I at least expected there to be some sort of hesitation on Gun's part, after all, this was to be the first time he had been separated from his mum Fly.

Gun just saw the open cage in Graham's truck, jumped in, curled up and went to sleep.

"Some bloody one man dog that is, you won't have any problems with this one."

And off they went, without a backward glance from either... charming!

The following weekend, Graham's faith in Gun was justified as he stormed home by a country mile to win the 6 dog race at Rendlesham, Suffolk. Gun had slotted into his team effortlessly and now the race Graham had picked Gun for loomed on the horizon, the twisty hilly terrain that had been chosen for the "British Championships"; The Forest of Ay.

Graham had been phoning me regularly with updates on Gun, so when the phone went Thursday evening I picked it up expecting it to be him.

It wasn't... but it turned out to be the phone call that literally changed my life.

"Alright Jim, Kirk here."

"Oh alright Kirk, how you doing, haven't heard from you for a while, what's up?"

"I've got a mother and daughter that I need to re-home, do you fancy them?"

Kirk was a musher of long standing, who predominantly ran Alaskan Malamutes, but over the years had finally succumbed to wanting the speed that Siberians gave you when running. So like all the "Johnny come lately's", relented and bought Zero dogs, the best that he could afford.

He had grabbed my attention big time.

"I take it you mean Siberians and not Mals?"

"Yes, roughly same lines as yours, all Zero with some of Woody thrown in."

"How old and what's wrong with them?"

"Mother, Charlie, is 5 and daughter Angel is three and a half. They've been passed from pillar to post these past 18 months, nobody seems to want to give them a permanent home, so could you?"

Kirk, had separated from his wife Jill and as so often happens, the dogs that they had owned jointly had to be re-homed as new partners rarely wanted to take on the remnants of the jointly owned pack.

Girls were a problem though, they would disrupt the male dominated pack which I had, but, and this was a big but, something clicked in my little brain, and without even consulting Cherry, I heard myself blurt out.

"Yea ok," trying to sound cool, "I'll give it a go, where are they?"

"Simon has them up near Heathrow, give him a call and arrange to pick them up"

"Kirk, one thing, are they still whole?" (Able to have pups)

"Yes, even the mother."

"Do you want anything for them?"

"No but if you breed I want either a pup or price of one. That OK?"

"Absolutely fine, thanks Kirk, I better give Simon a call and go get them"

Two days later Saturday 5th March, I met up with Simon next to the International Boarding Kennels that are sited there.

He pulled out the two girls, both tri coloured, and looking identical with a big white splash of fur on their left shoulders. They both looked beautiful, but I also noticed a few marks on the muzzle of what I presumed was Angel.

"Ok what's the problem with them, they look too good to be true?"

"Charlie is a fighter, she also bullies her daughter. You'll need to separate them if you keep both. If you only want to keep one, Angel is your best bet"

That meeting and bit of advice, although I didn't know it yet, was to later be the catalyst for my renewed interest in sled dog racing and all down to a homeless girl called Angel.

Chapter 15

Winds of Change

"What the hell have you done?" Cherry exploded when I opened up the doors to the truck and showed her the two dogs. "You're not keeping them, take 'em back were you got them from. They are not staying!"

Not exactly the reaction I was looking for, but what did I expect.

"They needed re-homing and I just felt sorry for them. Seven homes in 18 months. Don't worry, I'll find good homes for them."

"You better, and quick. I've had enough of this obsession with you and Siberians. I want a proper life, not one dominated by bloody dogs and sleds and rigs. Get rid of them."

Cherry's and my relationship was by now starting to fall apart. Her Landscape Design business was taking off, she was working longer and longer hours, and I didn't like it. My own career as an Area Manager for a Landscape company was also taking its toll on me. I regularly travelled over 150 miles a day checking on the many Landscape contracts I was running, mostly in inner London, and the strain was telling. Long hours, coupled with miles on the road do not mix, and it was showing in our relationship. It was falling apart.

What I should have done was take a step back, but I didn't. Don't know why, the solution was staring me in the face, but I just couldn't (wouldn't) see it.

"Well I've got them now. I'll sort something out, but for now I'll have to get them out the truck."

And with that, not even thinking of Cherry, I took Simon's advice and separated the girls.

Joker thought all his birthdays had come at once when I put little Angel in with him. He took one look, was completely besotted and started his courtship there and then. Sorted.

One down, one to go.

Took Charlie over to the furthest pen, and opened the door to introduce her to whoever she fancied. She had three to pick from. Labbie, Cougar or Dansa.

She chose Dansa.

And he wished she hadn't.

Charlie, walked straight up to him, and bit him... hard.

Dansa, startled and bemused, backed off sharply, blood oozing from his cut nose.

She walked over to Cougar.

Same outcome.

Pushing her luck, she walked over to Labbi.

Even at 14 years old Labbi was still a powerfully built dog, and Charlie had pushed her luck too far. Labbi had never backed down from anyone, and Charlie soon found herself pinned down, and I had to drag him off, before it really got out of hand. Cherry, meanwhile had watched all of this and repeated "get them out of here... NOW!"

It was at this stage I had to admit I'd pushed things too far, and quickly tried to calm her down by rapidly agreeing "I'll make a few calls, don't worry, Charlie will soon be gone".

Satisfied she stormed off, she'd got her way. Well she had 50% at least. Angel was going to stay. Joker was happy with his new playmate, I liked the look of her, just needed time to get Cherry to "see sense".

But who to give Charlie too? The solution came that night.

"Hiya Graham, how you doing?"

"We are in the lead just... and Gun was astounding. Even had to slow the rest of the team down on the down-hills, he was running that fast. He's superb. Don't suppose you'd consider selling him?"

"Come on Graham, you know better than that. Not at any price. Pups Yes, adults never, my name's not Pete." And both of us laughed at the mention of a guy who was renowned for trading in adult dogs.

"Tell you what though, might just have something you'd be interested in." And I related the tale of Charlie and Angel. I could sense his attention heighten when I told him the pedigree of the dogs. Again he had Zero's, and a breeding bitch was not to be turned down lightly. Besides as he already owned 20 plus dogs, one more was not going to make a difference in his set up.

"And you don't want anything for her. Just a good home?"

"Yep, that's the deal."

"Let me talk with Sue, and I'll get back to you. Don't give her away in the meantime."

Next day Sunday was not a good day for Graham. His totally reliable and fantastic dog Chalkie, slipped on the treacherous downhill section of the trail, lost vital seconds, and was beaten into 2nd place. Seems my luck went with my dog. Second again.

The next day Monday, we'd arranged to meet up again at Salisbury, and we exchanged dogs. No cloak and dagger stuff, though writing this, it sounds like a scene from a cold war film.

Graham seemed mightily pleased with Charlie, and Gun, to his credit, came over, gave me a big hug as he landed a sloppy tongue all over my face. He was forgiven for deserting me two weeks earlier, and off we went home, and Gun got the first look at his eventual mate, Angel.

Cherry had relented and said I could keep her. It may have had something to do with the sob story I told her, how nobody wanted her, a girl born on Christmas day , in a barn surrounded by shepherds and a donkey and... (Ok not really I made that bit up), but she changed her mind and Kiriak's Blue Angel had found her forever home. Now all I had to do was to get her to run. In all the excitement of picking the two dogs up, I hadn't really taken in any info about their running ability. I think I must have asked, but it had gone in one ear and out the next. All I could hear was Breeding Zero bitch... free.

Hooking her into the team on the Tuesday, I decided to take it easy and run the 2 mile loop at a gentle pace. Angel was only a small girl, and quite timid (who wouldn't be after the life she'd had?), so I wasn't expecting much from her. How wrong can you be, "don't judge a book by the cover" came to mind as she slotted in perfectly, and by the time we came into the home straight, was running in the team like an old timer.

As a season's finale, there was a very small meeting at Wellington Country park, only 2 miles in length, which we had run and won many times before, and I decided to enter a few teams.

Angel would be running at wheel with Fly and Dansa at lead, two very good leaders so all she had to do was concentrate on running. Trouble was it was very hot, too hot really to run the meeting, but as it was so short, mainly in the shade of trees, and twisty, meaning no flat out sprints, it went ahead. Dansa, being a heavy coated dog, did not like the heat, I could see him starting to get stressed after the first mile, and applied the brakes. We coasted home in 6th place, safe and sound. Joker and Gun meanwhile, having already shed their winter coats, carried on where they had left off weeks previously and stormed home to victory in 2 dog. So a 10 year old dog who was supposed to be retired (some hope) partnered by his year old Grandson had negotiated a very technical 2 mile trail, having over 20 turns, without missing a beat and winning with time to spare. I left the site a very chuffed and proud "musher"

But what of Cougar and his son Raider?

Raider was laid up having had a life-saving operation to correct a twisted gut. This is a particularly nasty condition that affects dogs that have small waists and eat quickly. Just the traits you want in a sled dog. But it's potentially fatal if you don't catch it and be operated on within the hour. Literally the stomach "twists" back on itself, the abdomen then "blows up" and the dog dies... painfully. The only warning you get is the affected dog starts to cough as it tries to catch its breath and the stomach starts to expand, alarmingly so. Luckily I had seen the signs after I had fed Raider and got him to the vets in time. He was saved... for now anyway.

Cougar's limp, meanwhile, had returned and he was now on medication from the vets. The bonus for me though was that I got to carry out the rarest of things, at least in the Siberian World. Labbi had given up running years ago, so to keep him active I used to walk him into the fields at the bottom of our lane. I gave up trying to use a lead as he would not, no matter how hard I tried, walk without pulling... and damn hard at that. So I just used to take him for walks off lead (Horror of horrors) and we had a great time. Cougar now joined us. As he had always been a bit timid (a trait of many Zero dogs), he would never stray far from my side. So each night would see me and my two Sibes leave the house and stroll down the lane, totally under control and not a lead in sight. This carried on for a month, me walking two beautiful Siberian Huskies in the summer, without a care in the world. Life didn't get better.

Then the pills wore off.

Over the weekend of 17th April, Cougar's foot had started to curl inwards and he couldn't straighten it out. Another visit to the vets was needed, so Monday morning, before work, I strode into the appointment room and waited. At this point I thought another course of tablets would be dished out. After all, it was only to be expected Cougar would have problems with that leg, DiMaggio having bitten it so hard in a fight that it necessitated a toe to be amputated years earlier. But what I heard next absolutely destroyed me.

"Oh, a heavily limping dog," Mr Vinnecombe, the resident vet said as I entered the consulting room.

"Yes, the tablets finished Saturday and he's started to limp again."

"Is he in any pain?"

"Funnily enough, it hurts him when you move his shoulder."

Mr Vinnecombe then touched the area, Cougar yelped, and he spoke the words that shook me to the core.

"If that's what I think it is, he's a goner."

"What?!"

"I think he's got cancer. He can't straighten his leg because the tumour is pressing on his tendon."

"So what's the cure?"

"Remove his leg," was the answer I didn't want to hear.

"You're joking aren't you?"

"No, sorry I'm not."

In total shock, I agreed to him being X-rayed to find out the truth. I left the vets with an anxious Cougar trying to get out, he really did not like to be separated from me. I went to work, which luckily was a site about 10 minutes away and awaited the news. And I realised that Cougar must have had this for months, what I thought was a limp due to an old injury was cancer. He'd been trying to run with the cancer growing inside him. It all made sense now. What a brave and courageous dog he was. And I knew what was coming when the phone rang.

"Hello Mr Bryde (never Jim, always Mr Bryde), we've X-rayed Cougar and it doesn't look good. It's 99.9% cancer. To be absolutely 100% we would need to do a biopsy. But both myself and Alan (the other resident vet) have reached the same conclusion."

"So what's the solution?"

"Operation to remove his leg."

And at this point I nearly fell over.

And then I found a voice from somewhere.

"You're absolutely certain?"

"Unfortunately yes."

"Don't bring him round. I can't do that to him. Lose his leg at nearly 12 years old. He's a top class running dog. No, let him go."

"You've made the right decision. So sorry Mr Bryde," and he put the phone down.

And with that, Cougar's life ended.

My big beautiful Cougar would be no more.

And so my trio of Zero dogs, Tupilaks DiMaggio, Bandit and Cougar, the dogs that had taught me the true meaning of "mushing" were no more.

I went through the next couple of months in a complete daze. There really was no talking to me, work was becoming a real bind, it was much too hot to train the remaining dogs and life generally was, as the French say "Merde".

And then on the night of Wednesday 25th May 2005, I watched, like millions of other people, enthralled as Liverpool came back from 3-0 down at half time to win on penalties in the most dramatic Champions League Final ever against AC Milan. I watched it on my own as Cherry was away visiting her brother, and by half time, was in a state of depression, much like most Liverpool supporters. Then the fight-back started, and as the goals went in, the level in my bottle of single malt "Dalwhinnie" went down. By the time of the final whistle, it was empty, Liverpool had won, and I think I went to bed a very happy man. Can't really remember , but I did arrive back at work the next day, where it seemed everyone on site had seen the game and was in as bad or worse state than me. Not much work was carried out that day.

But what it did do for me was make me see clear daylight at last.

I'd been with my firm for 15 years, made it to Area Manager, had worked on the most prestigious site in Europe "Disneyland Paris", and it was now time to move on.

The company had changed from what was a small family business when I joined, to what it was now, a rapidly expanding Landscape Firm, growing much too fast and after the "quick buck". We had been bought out by Capital Venturists, and they wanted results fast, and they wanted "yes men" on the team. I, was not one of them, and jumping before I was pushed, I left. But, me being me, I managed a very generous "golden handshake" on the way out.

As my sister has always said about me "If you fell into a pig sty you'd still come out smelling of roses."

I suppose she was right, because as well as the pay off, I started work for my new company the next day.

So things were looking up, it was now the middle of summer, the dogs were crashed out all the time in the pens, only coming alive to be fed at night, and I was starting to enjoy life again.

And it all came crashing down again on the morning of Friday 22nd July.

As usual, I would pop my head into the pens to say hello to the dogs before going to work. As by now it was warm most of the time, the dogs rarely stirred, preferring to just lift their heads up and give a little wag of their tails. Life really was so hard for them! And as you do you start smiling at their relaxed way of life, not a care in the world. Warm dry bed, nice bowl of meat and biscuits at night, the occasional walk, sunbathe all day, what could be better.

But Raider was not to be seen... anywhere. Odd, I thought and went to push the door to his pen open, and it wouldn't budge.

Raider, at 9 years old was dead.

He was bloated and it was obvious what had happened. The operation he had had some 6 months earlier for a "twisted gut" had not been 100% successful. I had been warned that it could happen again, and it had, with tragic consequences.

Raider in his short life had been a beautiful dog, and a very good runner, but he had a fatal flaw. He wanted to be Alpha male, and had a very nasty streak in him towards the other male dogs that I owned, particularly Joker. He'd inflicted a lot of damage in his time, had cost me at least two victories at Aviemore, but towards me was a very loving dog. Most other Mushers would have gotten rid of him years ago, palmed him off on some unsuspecting "newbie". I could never do that to one of my dogs, and I suffered the consequences. Suffice to say though, not many tears were shed on his passing.

Chapter 16

I Hear you Knocking

I now had 5 dogs, Joker, Dansa, and Fly who were all over 7 and considered veterans, and the two youngsters Angel, 4, and Gun 2. Not really much of a set up, so if I was to carry on racing, I would need to choose my races carefully.

We started off training in early September and the first race in the calendar was the old favourite Wellington.

Joker at 10 and a half was much too old now to be paired with Gun, so he was to run with his 7 year old son Dansa in the Veteran 2 dog class. Gun was to run in 3 dog with his 6 year old mum Fly with Angel at wheel. Despite it being unseasonably hot, we surprised everyone by winning both classes, and went home happy. We'd started off where we finished last season, winning.

The following month saw the launch of the very first 3 stage rally to be held in Britain. This would be a Friday night rally, Saturday morning over the same course and then move onto a new venue about 2 miles away for the final rally on the Sunday. The races were to be held up near Windsor on the Crown Estate and was eagerly looked forward to. Nobody had ever organised this type of event before, and it brought a very large entry.

As this was a new venture, nobody was sure how the dogs would react to three solid days racing, including myself. I now had to do some serious thinking about formations. There was no veteran class, so Joker would have to run against a lot of younger and fitter dogs. I felt that putting him in 3 would be too fast, so decided to pair him with my most powerful dog,

Gun. My gut feeling was Gun's power coupled with Joker's vast experience would get us home in the 2 dog class, with Dansa, Fly and Angel having enough speed to at least get a podium place.

How wrong can you be? In 2 dog we struggled. It was asking too much of Gun to compensate for having an ageing Joker next to him, and we eventually came home third.

Three dog however was a revelation. The 1st stage the night rally didn't go well, Dansa not really running well and stumbling quite a few times (I realised why a few years later, he was starting to go blind), but picked up the next two days where we slaughtered the opposition, winning overall by 2 minutes.

The following week saw us at The New Forest race, where having thoroughly learned my lesson, I paired Joker and Dansa in 2 dog veteran and Gun running with his mum and Angel.

We came home with two first places, with the two old boys, Joker and Dansa winning by the huge margin of 4 minutes.

Three race meetings, 5 first places and a third. A very impressive start to the season.

And that's where it ended.

Joker who was penned with Angel now started to get very amorous with her. As usual with this strain of Siberian, the bitches came into season only once a year. Now this would be fine if they had a bit of consideration for others, namely me and my racing season, but they didn't. Every year without fail, the girls would come into heat round about October, just in time to ruin the start of running.

Girls are a pain, even girl dogs are! (Joke) Once they come into season, the boys just go loopy. They lose all interest in running and sit there slobbering in their pens like some wino whose hit too much of the Aussie White you get from Yates Bar. It's pathetic really, these love sick dogs panting to get at the girls. And the girls make the most of it. Backsides shoved in the boys' faces, flirting with them, and then snapping like hyenas when they get too near. Sounds like a typical night out in Liverpool.

Anyway, I decided to stop all this nonsense and bring Angel into the house out of the resident "Lothario's" way... Jokerman.

Fat lot of good that did.

My 10 and a half year old pensioner, who should be on a deckchair sipping a cup of tea, decided otherwise. I heard a "scratching" on the front door, opened it and a mad looking Joker pushed past to find his "Angel". Looking across at his pen I saw what had happened. He had "eaten" a hole through medium grade weld mesh, pulled it back until it was large enough to crawl through and came a knocking on the door to see his girl.

Well, I wasn't having this, so back into the pen he went, and the mesh, bent back and a half inch sheet of marine ply hammered over the hole.

"That'll stop you, get out of that" and sometimes I really did think he could understand me. He just gave me a wicked looking grin, and ambled over to get some well-earned sleep, with I swear a "You are joking, think that'll stop me, think again!"

Next morning "scratching" at the door yet again.

I opened it and low and behold, there was Joker yet again. And yet again he pushed past me to get to his Angel. At this stage I should point out that this is no massive Rottweiler size dog with fangs the size of a tiger. This dog weighed at his best 21kgs. And yet he had the power of Hercules and a set of teeth like Jaws. The marine ply had been shredded as though by a beaver, and he had just pulled the wire back again, knocked on the door as you do, and waited patiently to be let in.

"Right you little bugger, you're not getting the better of me, I'll sort you out," and with that I took him outside and put him in the front seat of my pick-up truck and locked him in.

"Ok Houdini, let's see you get out of that."

Thirty minutes later, "scratching" at the door.

Opened it, and Joker, for the third, time pushed past me to get to Angel.

The side window of the truck was in shards on the floor. He had, I think, head butted it to escape.

"OK third time lucky, you win. I give up," as I put Joker back in his pen with his prize, Angel.

So we were going to have a litter of pups, Mr Joker had made the decision for us. Who's the head of this household? Obviously, not me.

And what of Joker. That randy old dog proceeded to mate Angel practically every half hour. There is one thing he didn't need and that was Viagra. What he did need though was a rest, and so did poor Angel; he would just not leave her alone.

The only thing I could do now was get her off the property, so I phoned up a mate who agreed to come and get her and keep her away until her season was over.

Joker watched Angel being put into a van and being driven away, immediately "cocked his leg," gave one of his resounding "howls" and ambled over to his box and fell asleep... job done.

And that is a lesson Siberian Husky owners get to know very well, nothing but nothing will stop a randy stud dog. Nothing!

The Date. Tuesday 24th November 2005.

Chapter 17

Angel

Training continued, running the 5 dogs up at Goodwood, until Angel became too big to train and on 8th January, I left her at home to prepare for the birth of the pups due two weeks later on the 25th January. Well that date came and went, and nothing, except I now had a Vietnamese Pot Bellied Pig waddling around the Pen. Angel was huge. And to cap it all, she flatly refused to budge from her own pen into the old barn I'd kitted out for her at the bottom of our garden. The night she was supposed to give birth I even slept in there with her, but nothing, except a very uncomfortable night's sleep for me.

I really didn't know what to do, so to take my mind off things I decided to go training with Hughie up at Goodwood. For a change we hooked up his 6 and my 4 for a 10 dog ride of our lives round the 4.2 mile loop. Being on the Quad gave us so much control that it was a pleasure to run such a big team, the old heavy cart I'd used previously now consigned to the scrap heap. A motorised Quad was the way forward from now on.

The dogs loved this as well, speed could be controlled, and we set it at 20mph for the whole route. By the time we'd finished everyone was happy, and Gun was so excited that when I let him off the line, he came over and jumped up to give me a big "kiss". That's what he called it anyway. Being so young he hadn't yet learnt to at least keep his mouth partly closed. I ended up with a French kiss with a difference, his canine tooth slit open my left eyebrow, and I was left with yet another battle scar. The hazards of owning Huskies.

Taking the dogs back home, I felt sure that given the peace and quiet, I would arrive to find mother and puppies, fine and healthy. What I got was an agitated Angel, pacing around her pen, obviously pissed off to be left alone yet again.

And then I had a brainwave. Put her in Joker's pen.

It worked, she settled down and started to make the sleeping quarters to her liking. Out went all of Joker's prized possessions, (in truth, a load of ripped up toys and a few revolting bones that he'd buried) and she made herself comfortable. She was happy, I was happy, even Joker was happy. He now got to sleep in the front of my truck. Settled.

And on 31st January, she gave birth to 5 healthy and very large pups, 3 boys and 2 girls.

Now the birth was over, I decided she had to go back in the stone shed. Joker needed to go back into his own pen, and besides, in the shed was a heat lamp that would keep everyone warm.

So I picked up the new pups, Angel followed, and soon she was happily lying under the heat lamp feeding her new family. All was well.

Next step was to phone up the people who had ordered pups to give them the good news.

First up was a mate Steve who had ordered 1 male. On learning that there were 3 males he immediately wanted two.

Next up was Charlie and Joe. Originally wanted 1 girl, now wanted the other one as well.

The only person who stayed the same was Max, and I think that was because all the others had gone and he was left with what he asked for, 1 Male.

However, I wanted to keep at least 1 pup, preferably a girl, so I told everyone I would confirm their orders the following week. And now came the fun part, naming the pups. Cherry and I already had a list of preferred names and this was quickly whittled down to Hobo, Bear and Jester for the boys. The list for the girls was thrown out of the window as they more or less picked themselves due to their markings. One girl had a white front, and black markings under her eyes... Panda. The other was born with a tiny white ring around her neck which showed up markedly against her predominantly black fur... Reef.

Watching them grow was a joy, 4 of them being very, very, playful and naughty, typical pups. However one pup, the big male, Bear, was proving to be very shy. No matter how much we tried, he just would not venture out of his box to play with his siblings. It also became painfully obvious that he wanted to be with his sister Reef, the only time he did come out he stuck to her like glue. So by default, Bear and Reef would be staying.

Eight weeks later, Steve came down to pick up 3 pups, his own and Panda and Jester who he would drop off to their new owners on route back to Yorkshire.

And while all was now rosy in the dog pen, my private life was going down the toilet... Even though I had a new job, it turned out I had jumped from the frying pan into the fire. What at first seemed like an ideal job, the landscaping of T5, the new terminal at Heathrow, was turning out to be one big headache. Literally! When I was younger I suffered a fractured skull, and it left me partially deaf in my left ear, which today is nearly completely deaf. That, I have been able to come to terms with. My hearing is perfect in my right ear, so I just turn my head and listen out of that. No big deal, lots of people have this problem. But the injury left me with a horrible affliction... tinnitus. Doesn't sound much (no pun intended here) but the continual ringing in your ear can literally drive you mad (and unfortunately, for some people it does). Over the years I have come to terms with this "white noise". Let's face it, I've had to as there is no cure. As long as you keep away from loud noise (standing next to speakers at a rock concert doesn't help) you are fine. So what do I do, take a job working under the flight path of the busiest Airport in the world. Not one of my best career moves! Coupled with the very long commuting I was having to do from Chichester every day, on that hell hole of a mobile car park that's affectionately known as the M25, I was not in the best of moods when my boss on site pulled me up over some trivial detail I'd overlooked.

I flipped.

I got into my car and left the site, and never returned.

I now had no job.

It was a couple of days before April 1st. April Fools' Day

But I was no fool, it was the best decision I'd made in years. The tension had now lifted off my shoulders. But it was too late to save our relationship. After 23 years together Cherry was going to follow her own Dream. She was moving to France... And I was not invited.

Once she had made up her mind, events moved like a steamroller. The house was put up for sale and was sold to the first people who viewed it. And at a very good price, this being 2007, at the height of the property boom. At least financially we would both be fine.

Cherry had by now decided to buy into a housing complex with another couple and turn it into gites. I have to admit this really pissed me off as I had wanted to do this years before, but Cherry had torpedoed the idea out of the water. But there was nothing I could do about it now, I just had to grin and bear it. The date for the sale was set for June 21st the longest day of the year. Ironic or what?

Chapter 18

You're Moving Out Today!

The days leading up to us moving out of Brook Cottage, meant we had to talk to each other as we sorted out 23 years of joint possessions. And we did just that, and through all the inevitable tears we both came to the same conclusion... we were making a terrible mistake. We did not want to part. Trouble was, now we had no choice. Cherry and the other couple had paid a non-returnable deposit on the complex in France. We had exchanged contracts, so had Frank and Shirley, Cherry's new partners. It would cost a fortune to stop the sales, and as I no longer had a job, the die was cast. No going back as they say.

By this stage I had no definite plans for the future, I was just going to rely on what I had always done all my life, hope and trust something would turn up. That something turned out to be 2 months in Scotland building dog kennels in exchange for board and lodging, for the girl who had bought a couple of pups from me years previously. Cherry and I both agreed that the time apart would do us good and as soon as she was settled in France I would come over and join her. Besides, at least in Scotland I would have somewhere to house my 7 dogs, and my Bengal cat. Cherry would be staying in a friend's caravan until the purchase of her place in France went through, nowhere near big enough to accommodate me and my tribe.

So Scotland that Summer, saw me and my constant passenger, Joker, travel the length and breadth of this most beautiful part of the British Isles. Joker for his part absolutely adored this, travelling with his head out of the passenger window taking in the sights to the astonishment and amusement of all who saw our passing. He and I would stop off wherever we fancied, usually within sight of one of the myriad of sandy beaches that dot the Highlands. There, I would wander along the shoreline, he would chase whatever he could see, and we were happy. Man and his dog. I even tried to compose a song in my head about this, but decided "me and Joker down by the shoreline" didn't quite match up to Paul Simon's classic "Me and Julio down by the school yard" so I left it where it should have stayed. In my head.

The Black Isle proved a real favourite with Joker though. He couldn't get enough of the place, and neither could I. To watch a pod of Dolphins flying through the air, catching Salmon is a magical experience and many a happy hour was spent on this pastime.

But all good things come to an end and as Summer finished, my thoughts turned to the long journey ahead, Confolens in the Poitou Charente region of France, about 1500 miles away. With 7 dogs and a perpetually whinging cat, this was not going to be an easy journey by any means. I was seriously looking at dropping China, as my cat is called, at Battersea dogs' home on the way down, that or giving her some gigantic sleeping pills to knock her out. Anything to keep her quiet. As it turned out though, she didn't make a murmur on the trip, think Joker must have tipped her off to behave or be out.

As it turned out she was the least of my worries.

Whilst reading one of the many books about "The Good Life In France", by any number of expats, Cherry had come up with a very little known fact about dog ownership over there. In short, if you live within 50mts of your neighbour, and that's measured from house to house, you are limited to a maximum of 3 dogs. Three Dogs! I had 7. This was not good news. And apparently if you did break the rules, and the local Marie, was, shall we say, un bastarde, the dogs would be confiscated, and you would then have problems getting them back. For the simple reason, you are only allowed a maximum of 3 dogs. A pure catch 22 situation.

Me, I did what any normal person would do, I Panicked. A Lot!

But once I calmed down I again did what I should have done in the first place, research on the web. Unfortunately, I found this little known fact is true, very rarely used, but can be, especially by any English and/or dog hating Mairie, the guy who has all the power in each commune.

I couldn't afford to risk this happening to me. Cherry had bought a commune of 3 houses with 3 acres of land. Plenty of space you'd think. But as is so often the case in France, her neighbour, even though English and had no objections to me bringing all my dogs, lived just 10mts from her farthest house. Even if he didn't object, someone else could. I just couldn't risk it. Not with the dogs at stake. I needed another solution, and quick.

I wanted to go to France, and I reckoned once over there I could get something sorted out. I just needed breathing space. Nothing for it, but to try and lend out 4 dogs to the racing community. They were all good running dogs and I didn't think I would have much of a problem.

First up was Steve, the owner of Hobo. He'd always wanted Bear, so he jumped at the chance. I tried to get him to take Reef, but he didn't want the disruption a girl would have on his predominately male pack. But he would take Gun. His friend and near neighbour Vicki would take Angel, and Charlie and Joe, who had bought Panda, would take Hobo's sister, Reef.

Dropping them all off at Steve's who lives in Yorkshire, was not easy, but I reckoned it was only going to be for a couple of months, so although upsetting, I knew I was doing the right thing. Couple of months is nothing. How wrong can you be? It would be a very long 18 months before I got them all back, a very long 18 months.

Chapter 19

Lost in France

Hooking up Joker Dansa and Fly, I opened the huge barn doors, called the command "hike on" and flew out onto the start of the track for our first training run in France. We'd arrived two days earlier, and I was determined to keep to the routine that had served me so well for the past 20 years, to train the dogs at least every other day.

Relations between Cherry and myself were far from ideal but at least there was a starting point now, we were in the same country.

Steve, who had my two dogs Bear and Gun, and his own Hobo, had elevated himself into British sled dog racing history. He'd travelled to Italy, and with Hobo leading, had won the IFSS version of the Dryland (rig) 6 dog World Championship. He had won the Nordic (pure bred dog) version of this race, and become World Champion. To this day the only Brit to do so. The other 5 dogs in his team were Joker's grandsons and granddaughters. To say I was proud was an understatement.

In the following year Steve ran Gun in various formations; 3, 4, 6, and 8 dog, and Gun won every race he took part in, 13 for the full year. An amazing achievement. With Bear now finally out of his shell and also competing on Steve's teams, he became unbeatable. He was now officially the best Musher in Britain. And I'd bred 3 of his dogs.

Joe and Charlie were also having a successful time, pairing Reef with her sister Panda and becoming the top all bitch team at Aviemore that year.

Angel, bless her was just Angel, enjoying her time with Vicki pigging out at her house whenever she managed to "flirt" her way inside, which apparently was more often than not.

The dogs I'd left behind were in good hands, Angel was enjoying herself. Suddenly I didn't feel so bad any more. They were doing what they were bred for, and by all accounts excelling at it; running.

Meanwhile my three oldies, continued their training, and were enjoying their new lives in France, particularly Joker who at 12 years old was now happily going for walks every evening with me around the local fields. What with his new found sleeping arrangements, the front seat of my truck, life was good for the dogs.

China my Bengal cat, meanwhile, was in her element.

Although wary of Huskies, particularly Joker, other dogs did not phase her one bit. In Scotland she'd terrorised my mates Alsatian, some feat seeing as how he was at least 10 times her size and weight, and encouraged by this, now turned her attention to our neighbours' two elderly greyhounds. As is the norm in France, properties practically touch each other and are usually only separated by the width of a road, front gardens being very rare in rural France. China loved this arrangement, as being at the end of a dead end lane, there was no traffic to worry about. Also the neighbours were a retired English couple, who loved cats and China was particularly striking with her marble markings. She also knew it and as is the way of most cats, played up to people all the time. But unlike most cats, she was not frightened of dogs, and would often attack any unsuspecting dog that she felt she could take on. Now she felt she had willing victims in the two greyhounds and soon she was making their lives a misery. She started to chase them. She had them so frightened that on one memorable day as she wandered into the back garden, they saw her coming and panicked, jumping into the swimming pool to escape. This was followed by a scream from Sue, their owner, who then jumped into the pool to rescue her precious pair of dogs. China, not phased at all, turned on her tail and swaggered back into our garden, head held high, proud of her day's work.

I should have warned her about the phrase, "what goes round comes round" because the next day it bit her on the bum.

As it was quite warm at night in the barn where Joker slept in the van, I'd started to leave the passenger door window open, ostensibly to make sure he had enough air. I knew he'd never run away, I just didn't think at his age he had the agility to jump out. I was wrong, and it was all China's fault. Coming into the barn the following morning I was surprised to find him curled up on the sofa in there. Thought nothing of it, until I heard a loud "meowing". Because of being deaf in my left ear it took me a while to get the direction this noise was coming from. Then I found it, China was 20 feet up a tree, and couldn't get down. Joker had obviously chased her up there. He'd restored the status quo... Dogs ruled OK.

Christmas and New Year came and went and I carried on following Steve's exploits on the web. He'd entered the IFSS World championships in Sweden in 8 dog. This was a major race, and being on snow, would be a test of his Sled handling skills. On the team were Hobo and Bear who were to lead, and Gun running directly behind in the position called Swing. Once in Sweden he realised that his dogs had not got enough miles on them in training for the 8 dog distance and dropped down to 6 dog. Despite this change in plans, he came home a very creditable 7th. Some going considering he was racing against teams that raced all year on snow. Steve, in England, got the chance to train on snow maybe 2/3 times a year. Yes that was some achievement.

Happy, he started the long drive home and it was only when he reached the ferry port in Holland that his mood darkened. Because I had planned to take all my dogs with me to France, I had carried out all the necessary procedures to get them there under the relatively new Pet Passport scheme. This involved a blood test for each dog, and once passed would allow you to bring your pet back to England. But there was a qualifying 6 month period. The phone call I received from

Steve that afternoon left me in no doubt that the Port Authorities had picked up on this.

"Jim, it's Steve. Can't get Bear and Gun back to England for another 3 weeks. It's either put them in Kennels over here or stay with them myself for the required time."

"Well, they are not going in kennels. I'll meet up with you and keep them here with me for the next three weeks."

"What about the 3 dog rule?"

"Don't worry about it, by the time anyone complains, and it's very doubtful they will, I'll have them back in England."

We very quickly made arrangements to meet south of Paris, where I would collect Bear and Gun and take them back to Confolens with me. I would take them back to Steve 1 month later when I was returning to England for a job interview. The couple who bought the complex with Cherry had not settled and had already moved back to England and the place was up for sale. Cherry and I were moving back to start again.

Both Bear and Gun went ballistic when they saw me, and it was a good few minutes before they calmed down enough for us to be able to load them up into my truck. Overjoyed at getting them back, we said our farewells and I drove through the night back to Confolens, a very happy man.

Bear and Gun quickly settled into their new home, Gun being made a fuss of by his mum Fly.

I had decided against running them, they were way too fast for my oldies, so ended up walking them instead. Gun loved this method of exercise, and took great delight in diving into the hedgerows to try and catch the very fast and elusive creatures that lived there... big green lizards.

He took great satisfaction in catching them, but couldn't get used to the fact that all he ended up with was a wriggling tail in his mouth and no body. The look on his face when the lizard ran away was priceless, he looked so stupid.

The three weeks passed oh so soon, and early May saw me back in England. I was interviewed and I got the job. It was a step down from what I was doing previously, but it paid well, and more importantly it was local, Portsmouth based. No more long hours on the road and a 3.30pm finish. It was ideal. It meant though that I would be living on a friend's farm in a caravan until I could find a suitable house to buy. This I didn't mind, but it meant I still wouldn't be able to keep Gun and Bear with me. Steve had planned his season around these two, and needed them to fulfil his commitments. He had entered the European Open in Holland and Bear was now leading his team with his brother Hobo. Gun was the powerhouse at swing. So, nothing for it but let him carry on as before, run the dogs in Britain's most successful and fastest team. I would just bask in the reflected glory.

Steve, being very astute, also realised at this time that if he wanted to carry on running, he needed more dogs, pups to be precise. And what better mating than a repeat of Joker and Angel. It had after all produced Steve's two leaders Hobo and Bear. Ok Bear belonged to me, but a repeat mating should produce the same result. Except for one glaringly obvious fault. Joker was now 12 years old, Angel was nearly 7 and this would be her last mating. If we were going to guarantee a successful mating, we needed a virile stud dog, and one was staring us both in the face.

Gun.

The mating took place and on the morning of 24th July 2008, Angel gave birth to her second and last litter. She had six pups, 3 girls and 3 boys.

I had buyers for the lot, even a waiting list in case somebody dropped out. The money would come in very handy and I was contemplating letting my mates have the loaned out dogs on a long lease.

But then I decided to go to Yorkshire to see the pups.

Big, big, mistake.

Vicki who had bred the pups had first option. She decided she wanted a girl and a boy puppy.

Steve wanted the same.

Louise, another friend had picked the remaining girl.

What was left was a black and white Gun lookalike, a boy Vicki had named Mole.

And I immediately fell in love with him.

"I'm having him Vicki, that's them all sorted"

And what I had done made no sense at all.

Bear and Reef were now 2 and a half years old.

Gun, his father was now 5 and a half years old.

I was back where I started, a completely unmatched team.

I either should keep the lot and campaign with a matched 6, or sell the lot.

What I was considering was madness.

But something in my little brain thought otherwise, and I kept him.

The name was quickly changed. It was either going to be Django, because I liked the name when I first heard it as a 7 year old in Birkenhead, or it was to be Duran, not after the rather limp band, but my hero and one of the greatest boxers ever. Roberto Duran. As usual Django was rejected by the Kennel club, (They had heard of the guitarist Django Reinhardt and rejected the name) but had no knowledge of Roberto, so Leahrno's Duran it became on his registration papers. But he answers to Django, and that's what he became. Django.

October that year, I went back up to Yorkshire and collected Angel and her new puppy Django, brought them back to my caravan and settled them in. I now had 5 dogs, and no team. The other 4 ranged from 12 down to 7, all far too old to form a team with this youngster. But, meanwhile I didn't have a care in the world. I had no bills coming in, apart from food, and I could play with my dogs as soon as work finished. Life at my age couldn't get much better.

Then the snows came early, and life for the dogs got even better. My caravan was parked up alongside Chichester canal and I had a 5 acre field full of snow all to myself. The dogs loved it. Out with the sled and round and round the field we went, having a ball. Once we tired of that, I would let all the dogs off, and for Fly this was the best part. The field was lower than the canal and so you had to walk up a little rise to see the water. This proved irresistible to her as she would run to the top, and slide back down. None of the other dogs could figure this out, and just stood and watched as Fly time and again went up the slope and slid back down again. Priceless. Angel and her pup, Django, just ran and ran, playing their own game of tag. And Angel was winning, her being very sleek now after the birth, and Django just a big ball of fat. But he tried and tried and Angel had great fun just being out of reach. Dansa, well his blindness was nearly complete, so he just stumbled around chasing shadows, because that's all they were to him. But he enjoyed himself and all reluctantly came back when I decided play time was over, and put them back in their pens to be fed and watered before I then took old grumpy out... Joker.

He never did live up to his name. When I let all 5 out for playtime, he flatly refused to join in. He just stood and waited by the caravan until playtime was finished, then and only then would he let me take him for a walk. Then we would do our daily walk along the canal side track, up to the city centre, I'd have a pint, Joker would have a half share of a packet of crisps and then we'd stroll back home, a round trip of 2 miles. Joker would quite happily walk alongside me, just about let the odd passer by stroke him, and always no matter what I did, run the final 200mts back to the caravan and wait for me to return. He would never try to carry on the extra 50mts which would take him onto the adjacent main road to Selsey. He would just run back and wait. In his old age he'd metamorphosed into a Labrador, there was no other explanation. Freedom called and he didn't want it, "Call of the Wild" meant nothing to him. White Fang... no chance.

But all good things come to an end. It was now getting cold, Caravan living is fine in summer, not so "hot" in winter. (Cherry had taken one look at the caravan, said no chance, and had decamped to a b and b, until the new house was ready to move into.) I'd found us a property in Selsey, a couple of hundred yards from the sea, and on 1st December 2008, Cherry and I were reunited at long last and moved into a brand spanking new 3 bed house. Life was getting better all the time.

Chapter 20

Aviemore 2009

Between Blue and Me

Steve had phoned me; he was planning to enter A (8 dog) class at Aviemore. This he explained was in preparation for the coming European Championships to be held in Holland in February. On a whim I decided I would go up and watch, expecting to make the trip alone. To my great surprise, and I suspect Cherry's also, she said she would like to come as well. So China went into the local cattery, and we packed up the remaining dogs into the truck. As we would also be taking Cherry's Border Terrier, Wizzy, Joker had to make the journey in the rear of the van in a box. Believe me when I say he made our lives a misery, there and back, a very long 1400miles. The front seat was **his**, not some stupid toy dog. His whimpering to let us all know he was displeased did not stop, and never again did I attempt this. The grief he gave both of us was just not worth it.

We arrived at Aviemore, minus my trademark entrance, Joker hanging out of the window to greet all and sundry. This got tongues wagging, as for the past 8 years everyone was used to seeing me and my shadow together.

"Where's Joker, he's not dead is he?"

I was asked this so many times that I relented, dropped Cherry off at a local coffee shop, stuck Joker back in the front seat and drove around for a bit with him sticking his head out to be seen by his adoring public. Pampered or what? Satisfied, he allowed me to put him back in his box, he'd made his point.

As we were staying with Charlie and Joe (who had Reef) Wizzy was allowed to stay in our bedroom and Joker got to spend his stay in the front seat as usual. I meanwhile made a beeline to see Reef, and got the shock of my life. She shied away from me, didn't acknowledge me at all, a total stranger to her. As she would be running the next day, I decided not to push it any further and left her alone. With this in mind, when I met Steve at the mushers' meeting that night I told him what had happened and told him I would not say hello to Gun or Bear until his race was run.

And it was at the meeting that I was met by the Club President, Paul Keen.

"Hi Jim, you're not entered are you?"

"No, just here as a spectator."

"Got any dogs with you?"

"Yes, why?"

"Want to do a bit of filming?"

"Yea alright. Who with?"

"See that guy over there, go and tell him I've sent you for the filming."

And over I went and introduced myself and at least get some idea what I'd let myself in for.

He explained that he wanted to film a race between a couple of Huskies and a Malamute. Did I have a couple of dogs that could do this? When I told him I had a couple of older dogs he said, ideal. Oh and one more thing did I have any experience of filming. Well this was my cue to impress.

"Yes I've done a couple of things."

"Oh, what?"

"Tomb Raider," I replied stone-faced.

"With Angelina Jolie."

"Yep, spent 3 weeks on set at Pinewood with my dogs."

"Well we're not as big as that, but you may have heard of us, Blue Peter?"

"Of course."

And then he outlined what he wanted. I was to supply two racing dogs and rig and train up the new girl presenter for a filmed race on Sunday. Now like everyone else of my generation, Valerie Singleton was Blue Peter. When I was introduced to the new one, I didn't have a clue who she was.

I was soon to find out. A very charming and very small, Helen Skelton.

Unlike Angelina Jolie, this person actually talked to us, and how. If you have ever seen her on the tele, that isn't an act. She is a live wire all the time, never shuts up.

She listened when I showed her how to hook up the two dogs, Angel and Dansa, showed no fear whatsoever when they took off down the trail with her hanging on like a pro. Needless to say, with all my expert training, (well I need the kudos), she won the race against the Malamute the next day... just. Dansa, taking no notice of cameras and crowds decided as only Huskies can that this was nothing new to him, and went for a number 2 half way round the trail. Just stopped dead and did his business without a care in the world. Helen unfortunately had a head cam on, and as she watched the whole episode, so did the viewers of Blue Peter. She filmed the lot in all its gory detail... charming. For the record she won by 4 seconds.

Later in the Cairngorm Hotel, Helen stopped by to buy me a drink and give me what millions of kids dream about, the coveted "Blue Peter" badge. Better late than never, even if I'm now nearer to being a pensioner than a teenager.

Thanking her, I then casually dropped a bombshell.

"Did you enjoy the race?"

"Yes, Dansa and Angel were brilliant."

"Glad you said that. Did you notice anything unusual about Dansa?"

"No, and apart from the toilet episode, him and Angel pulled very well."

"Well thought I'd better keep this till you finished. Not only is he 10 years old, he's totally blind!"

And her face dropped.

That was the highlight of the weekend for me... her face was a picture. Dansa and Angel had won, and she was happy.

Before all this, Steve had taken his 8 dogs to the start line and was looking good for a course record, all dogs fit and fast. Unfortunately, the trail was not up to standard. As had been the case the past few years, the trail was icy. The competitors had been warned about this at the mushers' meeting, but the dogs hadn't. Taking one of the very, very, fast corners, Gun had lost his footing, went down and was dragged by the rest of the team for quite a while until Steve managed to stop them. It was then a case of unhooking Gun from the team, picking him up (all 55lbs) and finishing the race with him under one arm whilst steering with the other. I'd missed the finish due to filming commitments, and rushed over to see Gun as soon as I heard the bad news. Opened up his cage and gingerly got him out for a close inspection. He had no major wounds, just some nasty looking scrapes that would soon clear up. This was the reality of racing on gravel. If it had happened on snow, there would be minimal damage, if any. We all knew this and we all accepted that accidents could happen. But the main thing was Gun would be fine in a couple of weeks. But his race was over. Steve ran a 6 the next day and won. Gun was not part of the team. But there was still another important race to be run; "The European Open". This was the race Steve had targeted, Aviemore was to him a training run in preparation for it. He'd based his season around this event, and bad luck struck again. During training on his trails in Yorkshire, Bear had sliced open his paw. This had needed 8 stitches and they were to be taken out the day before Steve travelled to Holland for the race. Bear was now an integral part of Steve's team, Leader with his brother Hobo, it was inconceivable to leave him at home. The solution we both came up with was simple. Double boot the injured paw. The trail in Holland was, as luck would have it, grassy, so the boot would last the distance. The Race Marshall was informed of what Steve would be doing, Bear was examined by the Race Vet before the start, and passed as fit. All would have been fine except for the light dew on the course as the race started. A very fast corner, the ground gave way under Bear's booted paw, and down he went. Up again within seconds, but the damage had been done. Steve was behind after day one. The next day he improved, but not enough, he came second overall. A very good result. But Gun was 2nd again, a finishing position that I was very familiar with. Would we ever win?

With the racing season over, something was gnawing in my mind.

Bear, had led Steve to an 8 dog Aviemore triumph.

Reef with her sister, Panda had led Joe to a 4th place and Top All Bitch success at the same meeting.

Bear and Gun had come 2nd at the Europeans.

I had Gun's son Django at my side.

That made a four dog team

I would have one more go at my Nemesis... Aviemore.

Chapter 21

The Trio Return

It was now May 2009 and my mind was made up. I wanted another crack at Aviemore C class. After coming second four times, I hoped five would be my lucky number. Fine you'd think, go for it. The problem, I didn't have a team. Well I did but three quarters of it was out on loan. A couple of phone calls would soon solve that problem, but I really didn't fancy making them. Although I had stressed when the dogs were originally loaned out that once I was settled I would take them back, their new owners Steve, Charlie and Jo, had fallen for them and hoped that I would relent and let them stay. That was never going to be the case, they had a home, and it was with me. Awkward phone calls made and a date was set. The following Friday saw me say goodbye to Cherry as I started on the, oh so familiar and, long route up to Scotland. Charlie and Jo lived just north of Aviemore, and I'd arranged to meet early the next day. Walking up to knock on their front door, I was not looking forward to this one little bit. The door opened and I was greeted by an already tearful Jo. This was not going to go well.

"Hi Jim, come in." Jo managed some sort of greeting. "Look we've really fallen in love with Reef, and she's happy here. She's really become part of the family. Are you sure you won't change your mind. We will give you top money for her."

"Sorry Jo, I realise you both have become fond of her, and I'm grateful that you helped me out by taking her in. But I'm even more fond of her, and she's coming back to make up a new team for me. Money doesn't come into it. Sorry, but she's coming home."

With that Jo burst into tears, Charlie and I both looked at each other, and shrugged.

Five minutes later I was driving back down the A9, with two passengers on the front bench seat for company. The ever present Joker and his daughter Reef. One down two to go.

"Alright Steve, I'm in Skipton town centre. How do I get to your place?"

"Stay where you are and I'll come and get you."

Ten minutes later I'm in Steve's front room.

"Look Jim, Gun is now knackered as far as my team is concerned, he can't keep up any more. Can't you just take him and leave Bear?"

"No Steve, sorry, I've come for both of them. Gun will be fine, he is going to run in 4 dog with Bear, so should be fine."

"Look you'll have problems getting Bear to run in a slower four. Anything below 12/13 mph and he trots. Won't even contemplate doing any work until he hits at least 14mph. He'll be wasted. He's used to running 8 dog now."

"Leave Bear to me, I'll retrain him, don't worry. But my mind is made up, they both come with me."

6pm Saturday evening I walked into The Seal Pub on Selsey High Street, ordered a Fosters for me and a white wine for Cherry, and collapsed into a comforting seat. Fourteen hundred miles, 2 hours sleep in 24 hours had taken its toll on me, I was knackered. I did however, have in my truck outside 3 very fast, tried and tested, sled dogs. At home, no more than 200mts away, sitting in his pen with his mum was Django, the 4th member of my new team. Tomorrow he would be introduced to his new team mates, Gun, his dad, and Bear and Reef, his half brother and sister. The Fab Four.

Next day I was up bright and early and arrived at Selhurst Park, Goodwood, by 8am. Excitement had gotten the better of me, and instead of my tried and tested routine of evening running, I was now like a young kid opening his Christmas presents as soon as day broke, which in a sense I was. Although I'd run and competed with Gun, many, many times, the other three were virtual strangers to me. Django was going to have a very steep learning curve, because apart from a few training runs with the older dogs, this was all new to him. He was going into a baptism of fire with three top class dogs, and at 10 months old, at least looked the part. Gone was his puppy fat, to be replaced with what would soon be even more evident, rock solid leg muscles. Although smaller than Bear and Gun, he was the same size as Reef, 21kgs, a very good fighting weight, Joker's weight to be exact. I was starting to dream!

"Ok buddy, you look like Joker, let's see what you've got," as I put him at lead alongside Gun.

"Lead? Jim, you've just put Django at lead. You sure you know what you're doing?" Hughie politely asked.

"Hope so, Hughie. Figured Reef and Bear would go too fast and frighten him, Gun I can control. He at least understands easy (slow down)." and with that I released the brake, and prayed. The first 50mts or so I was thinking I'd made a mistake, and then the "light-bulb" switched on in Django's head and we motored. For the rest of the 2 mile loop the dogs ran in total unison, Django matching his old dad Gun's stride perfectly, the image of Great Grandad Joker. And as we finished Hughie asked,

"How did he go?"

"We're going to win Aviemore, that's how good he went."

Despite this more than promising start, I needed Django to "learn" his craft. The speed was obviously there, as was the attitude. Those two attributes are brilliant, but without a third and very vital one they are virtually useless. He needed to learn his commands, for without them, all you've got is a very fast team going nowhere. Even the slowest team on the planet will beat you if you don't turn when you're told, something that eventually dawns with even the dimmest musher. And I had some of the best teachers around, Fly and Dansa.

Dog running is not as hard as it seems, the dogs do virtually all the work, and the musher gets the credit. That's wrong, the lead dogs should get all the credit, for without them you, the musher, are nothing. And to have a proven leader is priceless.

When you first start "Mushing", unless you have bought some older dogs, it's like the blind leading the blind. Nobody knows what to do, and tangles and curses abound. Eventually, if you are lucky, one of your dogs is smart, picks out of the chaos what is required and eventually gets to lead the idiot behind on the rig around the trail to the finish. Once you have one leader, he/she will teach the dog alongside, and so on ad infinitum. You just have to find your lead dog. And if you are really, really lucky, once in a lifetime you get a dog who is a complete natural. Joker was that dog for me. He was running lead at 7 months old and never ran anywhere else. All my other dogs eventually learnt from him, and he taught them well. Fly and Dansa were his offspring, and were excellent leaders. Now it was time for them to pass on the mantle and teach the young prodigy, Django, the ropes.

With the weather now turning hot, short sharp training runs were the order of the day, 1, maybe 2 mile max. With Angel making up the 4, runs were smooth and turns perfect. Not too fast, not too slow, just a good steady pace, the advantage of owning older and very good reliable sled dogs, priceless. It was a joy to run, calm and steady, take in the scenery, read a book even, no problem at all. Perfect.

Then the mood changed, the lunatics went on.

Gun, being older and sensible, for a dog anyway, was no problem to hook up at the start. As long as you didn't mind him growling at you before jumping into your arms from the top tier of the dog truck, into your "better be ready" arms, you were fine. Put him up lead and he would stretch the line out taut and wait for the rest to be hooked up.

Same couldn't be said of Bear and Reef.

Both had to come out together, and once out would twist and turn and try and smell/eat the grass, go for a toilet break, any number of things other than what was expected of them... line out... straight. Whichever one you put up front next to Gun, would immediately turn round to be with the other as that one was put at wheel. To this day they are still the same, even at nearly 9 years old, and it is a pain. But eventually you get going and then you notice that Reef is dragging her heels. She wants to go to the toilet and won't run flat out till she goes. So you stop the team, she does her business, looks back, gives a look that says "I'm finished now, we can carry on" and then goes into warp speed. And this palaver never happens on race day, only training, and they say dogs don't have a sense of humour!

So we are now doing the equivalent of Mach 1, or feels like it. All the dogs are stretched out and moving like greased lightning, we're flying, and this goes on as long as we are on the long straight flat part of trail. We go through the car park area, thankfully empty, and hit the 180 degree bend where we have to slow, round it and the trail rises up. Reef and Gun are still trying to gallop, Bear, as Steve had predicted, drops into a walk, (trot) at 13mph. I can't even run that fast, flat out and here he is, this bloody dog, walking. Now this is fine if you want your dogs to run the Iditarod, in fact it's what those mushers aim for. A fast trot eats up the mile effortlessly; ask the Wolf.

But we were not running the Iditarod, we were sprint racing, and I needed the dogs to gallop, run flat out. In this gait the dog is at its most powerful stride, pulling and running as it was bred to do. If I let Bear carry on trotting, we would get round Aviemore very easily, but very slowly. I needed to break him of the habit.

"Bear, hike on." Nothing, not a bloody thing.

"Bear, if you don't bloody hike on you are going to Mount Noddy's (RSPCA Dog Pound) on the way home. I'm not kidding, bloody hike on." (Like he understands, right?) No response whatsoever.

"Bear HIKE ON," as Bear continues his walk and looks back and grins as he wants to know what all the fuss is about, still bloody walking.

"Whoa" as I pull the brakes and stop the team.

Immediately Bear starts straining into his harness, I call "let's Go" and we lurch off again at the warp speed we'd entered the hairpin at, Bear pulling and running as hard as the other two.

I spent all that summer, stopping and restarting the team whenever Bear, broke into "the Walk." I pleaded with him, promised him extra food, a night on the tiles, a visit to a pole dancing club (ok I exaggerate a bit here, but not much) It didn't work. To this day if the speed drops, he still goes into what is known and desired amongst long distance racers as "The Iditarod Trot". Ideal for travelling 80 miles a day, useless for the much smaller distances covered by the sprint racer.

Bear, to his credit obviously didn't think he was doing anything wrong, his "walk" was keeping him up with the other two. So the only solution was, pretty obvious really, don't slow down. And that in a nutshell is what I've done ever since, run them flat out. They are happy, I'm terrified at times, but we win. And that's what it's all about.

By now it was the beginning of September and thoughts were turning to Aviemore. The weather was turning cooler and I needed to start serious training. Dansa was finding it extremely difficult to keep up with his team mates, so I made the decision to run him solo. He was totally blind by now, but amazingly still wanted to run. And from then on he became a bit of a star. People could just not get their heads around seeing an 11 year old dog pulling around a twisty 2 mile trail on my racing rig and being told "He's Blind" After they picked their jaws up of the ground I did explain that he knew the course, and even though I gave him the required commands, "Gee, Haw, Straight on" he was already turning before he heard them. They say a dog's most important sense is smell, and here was the proof. Dansa, by turning before my command could obviously smell the trail he'd left previously. An amazing, amazing, dog.

With Dansa sorted, that left me with 6 dogs that all needed to be trained. With Angel and Fly not really being the best of mates, I decided to train the lot, together.

Fly and Gun at lead, Angel and Django at swing, Bear and Reef at wheel. No fighting, no arguing, guaranteed, for the simple reason, that's how they were penned. Let the brake off on the quad, ran the 2.6 mile loop, and my mind started whirling. They were fast, bloody fast. Six dog Aviemore?

Fly would be 10 years old in two weeks and the idea was soon binned. She was much too old for a fast 6. You may get away with a one day race, but two hard days over the stony Aviemore course? No back to reality. Four dog.

The first race of the season, Buttersteep, near Windsor was on Sunday 11th October. As it would be Django's first outing, I decided not to scare the pants off him and run him in a four with his mum and brother and sister. Gun and his mum would run in the two dog. All families together... aah. Sentimental to a fault, me.

Two dog off first and home in a rubbish 5th place. Whilst Gun was as usual frantic, Fly looked at me, the set up, and before we even heard "Go", I knew I had made a mistake. She refused to play ball and walked around the course, had her water and sulked for the rest of the day in her box.

Django was paired with Reef at lead in the 4. Despite being very nervous at the start, to such an extent everyone thought he'd refuse to run, he eventually settled down and we finished 2nd. For a debut this was fine, on the podium first time out, not bad at all.

For the next month we trained as a 6 dog, swapping leaders to find the best combination. We entered another Rally, came 3rd over the 2 days, Django and Gun in lead in the 4 dog, and generally things were going as planned. Use the rallies as training days in preparation for Aviemore C class in January. All was going well, you'd think?

Reef decided at this point to throw a spanner in the works and come into season, and was quickly despatched to the local Boarding Kennels. Normally this occurred in September, before really serious training had started, not two weeks before Christmas, brilliant, brilliant timing, Thanks Reef, You're a Star.

Bear immediately went into serious decline, with his litter sister missing he had as much pull in him as a soggy rice pudding, he was useless.

Dansa, on the other hand, perked up and started acting like a Casanova. I hadn't taken Reef out early enough, he could still smell her and had turned into a gibbering wreck, a blind one at that. At least the other males could see she wasn't around, he couldn't. To him she was in the next pen, and more importantly, available.

This proved disastrous to Django. He was penned with Dansa, and still being very young, had no idea what the problem was. He just saw a rejuvenated playmate and decided to take advantage. Dansa, to his credit did give a couple of warning nips to the youngster, but Django was too thick to understand. He decided he didn't like getting nipped and gave Dansa one back. And that one nip ended my Aviemore dream for that year. Dansa, being an Alpha male could not let this youngster question his authority and wallop, bit the nearest bit of body available, Django's front right leg, and hung on.

I heard the screams, came running out, and shouted at Dansa to "leave it", and to my utter amazement, he let go. But he had left behind a big bloody mess of a foreleg, and a very, very frightened Django. He'd just learned a very valuable but harsh lesson, one that all young pups eventually come to understand. Don't mess with the Alpha male.

Knowing Huskies as I did, this also meant that the two dogs would need to be separated from now on. Django may be frightened now, but eventually he would exact his revenge, law of the jungle and all that. And Siberians, as I had come to realise, had very long memories.

Dansa was put on his own into a pen next to the others, and to this day at 16 years old is happy and contented in his own kingdom. At least some good came of the fracas.

Django's injury was X-rayed when the swelling went down and the news was not good.

"I'm afraid he has a minute chip out of his tibia, not much but you need to rest him, no running at all for say a couple of months. Keep him quiet."

Django had had enough of this examination by now, wrenched himself free, jumped off the table and headed out of the open door.

"Keep him quiet and no running for 2 months, you're joking aren't you? He's a young dog at the peak of fitness, you tell him he can't run!" And with that I went outside, collected

Django and went back home and tried to figure out what to do next. There was no way I could keep a 17 month old Siberian still and quiet for the next 3 months. Maybe, just maybe if it was hot, but it wasn't. It was December. And, it had just started to snow! Not a snowball's chance in hell.

But that snow was, as it turned out, a blessing in disguise.

Because I lived only 200mts from the sea, any snow that fell would be melted and turned to slush within hours. Sehurst Park, was situated on the crest of the South Downs, a few hundred feet higher, and 15 miles from my house. That made all the difference. The temperature difference was such that any snow that fell here could and often did remain for weeks. And this fall was particularly heavy. It was going to settle. Running on fresh snow would be ideal for Django. There would be a cushioning effect, and if I ran the dogs in small teams, two's/three's, the speed would be relatively slow. Django would get his exercise, he wouldn't be stressed; things were working out. There was one small problem in my thinking though. Selhurst Park was situated between the two main routes over the Downs leading out of Chichester.

The Eastern route went past the famous race course Goodwood and on to Midhurst. The western route went past The Rolls Royce factory and on to Petworth. These two arterial routes would within hours be clear of snow, having been salted. The road joining the two would still have the snow, it wasn't considered prominent enough to be either salted or snow ploughed. And my training ground was smack in the middle.

"Snow, Snow everywhere but never a drop to sled"; Rhyme of the ancient musher.

But you can't keep a good musher down, and undeterred I loaded up the Danler sled, all 7 dogs and took the Petworth road. As I thought, it was totally clear until I came to the turning for my training ground. Here the road was indistinguishable from the verges. Just pristine white beautiful snow.

"Snow, snow everywhere bla, bla, bla," goes the poem.

And then the miracle happened. Ok not quite, but this is the truth.

"Alright la, you stuck, need a tow?" A familiar scouse accent came out of the driver's side of the snow plough that had just pulled up.

"Knackered mate. Got me dogs in the truck and can't get to my training ground about 1 mile along that road. Sold my 4 wheel drive and bought a bloody transit instead!"

"Listen la, this is your lucky day. How about I flatten the snow along the road for you?"

"What!"

"Yea, no sweat, get your own pisted run. Hook up the dogs and follow me."

Turns out the guy had loved sled dogs all his life and had even had a go up in Sweden a few years ago. This was too good an opportunity to turn down.

"You're on, give us a couple of minutes. Ta mate."

Without even thinking of the consequences, I hooked up Dansa, Fly and Angel, the slowest dogs I owned, pulled the snow hook, and flew, along the main road. Unbelievable, a man, all-right an idiot, 3 huskies and a boat, (no that's not right); a sled, a supa dupa all singing and dancing Danler sled, travelling without a care in the world in the wilderness of West Sussex. Who needs Alaska? The sky was bright blue, the sun was shining; I could be mistaken in thinking I'd been magically transported to the Alps. Out into an opening I saw in the distance, the sea calm, still and shimmering, Bognor Regis never looking so beautiful, and me and the dogs "lovin' it".. At this point I wouldn't have swapped it for the world.

Carrying on we went back into the tree cover, down a dip in the road and I called a gee as we swung right and under the barrier (just) as we entered familiar territory, my training ground.

Immediately, Dansa's ears pricked up as he realised where he was, the start of the 2.6 mile loop. I called another gee but he and Fly were already turning, they knew exactly where they were. Now, travelling became very tough and hard going. Whereas we had had the luxury of a flattened trail on the road, now we were on pristine virgin snow, and it was over 18 inches deep in places. Beautiful to look at, a real picture postcard scene in fact, but terrible to travel on. It's at times like these when the breeding of the Siberian comes to the fore. This is their true home, not the gravel tracks we use in Britain. Dansa and Fly, both had a quick mouthful of the white stuff, settled themselves into their harnesses, and pulled; hard. They were back in Siberia, welcome home. Dansa, was in his element. His blindness was not a hindrance here, there was nothing to see; it was all pure white, as is he. On and on he and Fly ploughed, maybe making at best 8 mph past the Electricity Pylon that signalled the left hand turn down to the Northern limits of the trail. We wouldn't be taking that route today and I called "straight on". On through the deserted car park and up to the 180 degree hairpin bend. Here we always went left and basically did a loop and went back down the trail we had just come up. Not today, we would go right, the main road we had just travelled on being no more than15metres away.

"Gee Dansa, Gee."

We took a "haw".

"Dansa gee!"

Nothing, he and Fly went left.

"Bloody dogs," as I placed the hook, jumped off the sled , went to the front of the gang line, grabbed the neck line tying Dansa to Fly and dragged them round and placed them in the direction I wanted them to go.

"You go straight ahead here Dansa, Straight ahead" and I went back and jumped on my sled.

Dansa and Fly were now back where they started, looking down the regular route that they always travelled.

"Gee Dansa Gee." Fly to give her credit, tried to go right, but Dansa was having none of it.

"This is where we go left, we always go left, I'm going left" you could just imagine that thought going through his bloody head.

We could still be there now, me jumping off, dragging him round, getting back on the sled, him back where he started, and he would have won. A more determined and stubborn dog you will never meet.

This could go on all night, I would be calling Gee while he would go left, ad infinitum. Nothing for it, get off and drag the dogs onto the road. And that bloody dog fought me all the way, until his feet hit the icy road. This was unfamiliar territory for him, so he quite happily took the command, "hike on" and trotted back to the truck, a very happy and contented dog.

The snows lasted for about a week and I was up there every day, making the most of my good fortune. The only alteration was I never went into the woods any more, just turned them on the road, going back the way I had come, Dansa had won. Because there was only a very thin covering of ice on the road, steering and control of the sled was practically non-existent, the runners had nothing to bite into. For this reason running small teams was the only way to go, putting a 6 dog on would be suicidal, a truck coming the other way at speed didn't bear thinking about.

But luck was with us that week, traffic was practically non-existent, and if a car did pass us, it went past slowly, we waved, the passengers were goggled eyed and everyone smiled. The Land-Rover I saw coming towards us that last day therefore didn't cause us any alarm, we would do the same as usual, smile and wave and carry on the run. Only there was something odd about this vehicle, it had a blue flashing light. And getting closer I noticed it also had nice blue lettering along its side "Police".

"Oh shit, I'm in trouble here," as the vehicle pulled ever nearer.

I was already mentally preparing my excuse.

"Sorry officer, the bloody dogs saw a deer and chased it out onto the road, and I'm just trying to get back onto the trail" sounded reasonable.

"Hello sir, enjoying ourselves are we?"

"Er yes," as I recognised the driver. He'd stopped me a couple of times before when I was training alone in the woods.

"We've been travelling along here for the past week and couldn't work out what was causing the two parallel scratch marks on the road. Looking at your sled we've solved it, your brake marks. Have a nice day" and drove off. And I didn't get nicked. Aren't our coppers wonderful?

The next day, just after I rounded the first bend, there it was, another Land-Rover. I thought I wouldn't push my luck again so I started to turn around when I noticed something odd. It wasn't a copper coming to the rear, but a young lad carrying a pair of skis. I watched amazed as he put them on, grabbed hold of a rope that was tied to the rear bumper, gave a thumbs up, and took off, The Land-Rover towing him down the road. And I thought that what I was doing was nuts! Just another day in Conservative boring West Sussex.

Chapter 22

Run Like the Wind

Aviemore was now well and truly put on the back burner. Although we had had fun on the snow, running small teams over short distances was no preparation for the race. Instead, cutting my losses I teamed up with Hughie to practise overtaking along the twisting trails of Selhurst Park.

The idea was I would run my fast three, Gun and Reef in lead, Bear at wheel and Hughie would run the remaining 8 dogs, putting Fly and Django up at lead. With him running a much slower team, it was easy for the two of us to get him off first, and then I would hook up my three and give chase. We usually caught him after a couple of miles, when I would call trail, overtake and then race for home. This not only gave overtaking practise, it also gave his lot the opportunity to pick up speed and run fast. Perfect, why doesn't everybody train this way? Well the following Sunday, with the snow well and truly gone, we found out the hard way.

Joining us was a mate who had a single Siberian that he wanted trained. This was not unusual, as we frequently had people phoning us up wanting to come training. Usually, they only came a few times and we never saw them again. They saw what we had achieved and thought it looked easy (it wasn't, it was years and years of hard work). Once it dawned on them that it took more than a couple of training runs, they gave up. But this lad had stuck with it, and I was starting to trust him.

Big mistake.

This particular day I'd asked him to hook up the dogs, and to put Gun on first. This, I explained to him, was because he could be guaranteed not to turn around and attack whoever was behind him. He would hold the gang line tight, and so, no tangles, no fights. As I trained on my own mid-week, this was vital for me. Trying to untangle a fighting 6 dog team was not to be recommended to anyone. So whilst I helped Hughie hook up the other 8 dogs, I was confident that he would cope. He didn't. Whilst he did as I asked him with Gun, he didn't watch what was happening with the other two dogs, Reef and Bear. He apparently was too interested in watching what we were doing, and took his eye off his own team.

Hughie let the brake off, Django and Fly took off down the trail and I strolled over to my, by now, 3 frantic dogs, they were screaming to get going. Normally, I'd double check everything before setting off, but I too was preoccupied, I was looking down the trail to see how Django was performing.

Second big mistake.

"Hike on boys, let's go get 'em," as I let the brake off. They flew down the trail desperate to catch Hughie. Speed, as well as overtaking training, what could be better?

"Look at the speedo, 23mph already," I said over my shoulder, "We'll soon catch Hughie."

The first right hand bend was looming up and I was feathering the brakes to slow us down, when something odd caught my eye. The main gang-line seemed very long, odd. And then alarm. Running alongside the gang-line was an elasticated section... a Bungee. This acts as a shock absorber, saving the dogs' shoulders from injury. And looking at it now it was fraying fast. The dogs had nearly bitten through it. It was holding, just. I slammed the brakes on.

"Paul, get off quick and grab hold of Bear, quick."

He was off in a flash, and made a desperate bid to grab Bear.

Too late.

The three dogs, wanting to chase, slammed into their harnesses, the last few strands of bungee parted, and goodbye team as they rapidly disappeared down the trail.

"Paul, see you back at the truck, I'm going after the dogs" and left him standing there open mouthed as I revved up the quad and roared off down the trail. I knew from bitter experience that they would run the same route we'd been running the past two weeks, that would be fine. It was what they would meet on the trail that worried me now. Selhurst was full of Deer, Badgers, Pheasants, and the worst of the lot, pet dogs running free. Disaster loomed. I went even faster, and then saw them up ahead, they were bloody moving like the wind, flying. But I also saw another figure up ahead… Hughie.

I started tooting my horn, but nothing, he couldn't hear us, his own engine drowning out the noise. Eventually though, he did hear, and looked around. And bearing down on him was my out of control team. Hughie, bless him, immediately took in what had happened, stopped his team, quickly dismounted and caught Gun and Reef by the neck line as they thankfully slowed down for him. I was with him in seconds and working quickly, soon had my lot hooked back up to the front of my Quad, ready to resume training.

"Hughie, where's your Quad?" as we turned and saw an empty space in front of us.

Third big mistake.

Hughie had forgotten to put his handbrake on, and his team had just taken off without him.

"Jump on Hughie, we need to get to them before the hairpin."

We shot after the runaway team, and saw to our relief that they had stopped, the Quad had run into a ditch, just before the nasty bend, guaranteed to tip over a driverless Quad. The consequences of that happening didn't bear thinking about.

"Bloody hell Hugh, that was lucky."

"Jim, Fly and Django are gone."

Fourth big mistake.

"Oh F.....k I'll have to find them, see you later," as Hughie quickly dismounted and I took the left hand bend, just in time to see Django and Reef take the right hand bend up ahead. If they followed the trail they had been running, they would reappear onto the main trail about 30mts ahead, the route they'd taken doubling back on itself. I waited and sure enough they emerged and then it was a very simple task to get them to follow me home... safe.

First thing right all day.

Hughie came in some 10 minutes later, all remaining 6 dogs, fine and sound.

And what had happened?

Fifth big mistake.

Dansa, who we had put in at swing had become impatient and bitten through the gang-line in front of him, thereby releasing Fly and Django.

And me and Hughie.

Forty years' experience between us and 5 stupid mistakes.

Rookies!

Chapter 23

Jokerman

Django's leg was slowly improving and by the 1st March he was back running lead next to his dad Gun on the 4 dog team, and running even faster. The season's final race was 2 weeks away and I decided to give it a go. As it turned out it was a very warm day, much too warm really, and I eased the team home to a 2nd overall. And so for the first time in my career as a sled dog racer, I ended the season having not won a race. We had had some good fast training runs, but had not yet been able to transfer that to race day .Even though I had some very good fast, experienced dogs on the team, they still hadn't gelled as a unit. Django's injury had played a major part, so to get him back fully fit was a bonus. As the season was now finished, it was a summer of fine tinkering with the team that lay ahead of us.

But as summer approached, instead of looking forward to it, I was dreading it.

Joker, my dog in a million was approaching his fifteenth birthday. And, without me really noticing, he had aged rapidly. Last November he had surprised everyone at training by jumping out of my truck and racing after me down the trail, chasing his offspring, at 14 and a half years old. Now, just over 4 months later, he was finding it difficult to get up and go to the toilet. This meant he could no longer clean himself properly, and with the weather getting warmer by the day, this spelt trouble. He was a dignified old boy, a very faithful dog, my best friend, and I couldn't stand by and let this happen to him. I had to do what was best for him, feelings couldn't be allowed to interfere with what I had to do.

Tuesday 25th May, just 41 days before his fifteenth birthday, I took my beloved leader for his final walk.

I held him in my arms as the vet administered the fateful injection, and I carried him back outside, tears streaming down my face, unable to utter a solitary word. I placed him carefully on the front seat where he had decided to live for the past two years, and drove up one final time to the training ground where we'd spent so many happy years together.

I think I sat there for a couple of hours, talking to him, looking down at the coast line of Chichester Harbour, trying to compose myself for what I had to do next.

I had already phoned the crematorium the day before so they knew I would be arriving before midday. I handed him over without a word, I just could not speak.

Two days later I made the return journey to collect his ashes. I drove straight to Selhurst Park, got out of the truck, and said my farewells as his ashes blew down the trail.

Tupilak's Joker. 5th July 1995 – 25th May 2010.

Chapter 24

Shadow on the Wall

Everyone has heard the phrase, "trouble comes in threes" and usually it is something trivial that triggers the recollection of it. But the third trouble came with a mighty bang, and made me question my future within the sled dog world.

Angel for the past day had not eaten. Nothing really unusual in that, she often didn't bother at meal times, and Django benefitted by having two meals. But there was something odd about Angel this time. Not only was she off her food, she was sulking in the corner of her pen, very listless. Nothing for it, I would have to take her to the vets, see if they could sort her out. Next day I went to collect her for the visit, called her over and she flew over to me, jumped up into my arms, and gave me a big kiss. "Ok girl, no vets for you, so what was the problem, tummy bug?" I asked, half expecting her to answer. Instead she wandered over to the far corner of the pen and froze.

"Ok what's the problem?"

"What the hell is that?" as I saw what she was looking at.

Lying on the floor was an odd cigar shaped object.

Kicking it, because let's face it, dog muck is not very nice, I caught sight of its colour, yellow, "fifty disgusting shades of yellow."

I remembered then. I'd noticed that one of my leads was missing the end part, now I knew what had happened. Angel had chewed the end off, and swallowed it. It had passed through her system in two days. She had been a very, very lucky girl. It could have killed her.

Now that she had regurgitated the offending object, Angel was fit again to run, which was a relief to us all, including the newest member of "our gang", a Portsmouth lad, Don. He'd been training with us for about a year now, had his own two dogs, which raced with Hughie's team most of the time. He did however have a soft spot for Angel, so it was with some relief that I could tell him that she was fine.

"Listen Don, as Angel has recovered do you want to take a big team out?"

"Yea ok mate, Hughie coming with me."

"We'll get him to follow on his quad, in case you get lost." I replied without a hint of irony.

"Yea, funny."

"Well it's not your fault you come from Pompey. Once over the bridge and you lot get lost. That's what Island living does for you" Portsmouth being connected to the mainland by two bridges, so it is in effect an island.

"Look I've only gone wrong twice up here, that's not bad."

"But we had to send out a search party for you, International rescue was on standby as well," piped up Hughie. Don by this time knew he was beaten, shrugged his shoulders and got on with hooking up the team, and we let it lay there.

"Don't let them go too fast Don, just take it easy," I said to Don, "And smile as you pass me," as I ran up the trail to get into position. Today I was going to be David Bailey.

"Hike on," shouted Don, struggling to be heard above the noise of 11 screaming huskies, led by Fly and her son Gun.

They came back some 15 minutes later, all safe and sound, and we inspected the photos I had taken. One was an absolute gem. Gun and Fly straining at the gang line, power personified.

"How old is Fly Jim?" Don asked.

"11 in September."

"And she can still run like that, Brilliant."

And that was the last photo I took of her.

Two days later I was back up the woods and running a six, Fly and Gun again leading the team. The weather was seasonally warm, but they ran beautifully, matching each other stride for stride, running the 2.6 mile loop with the ease that only Siberians can.

"Good dogs" I said to them as I put them away. "One of our best runs ever. You were brilliant Fly. Not bad for an old girl." I was grinning from ear to ear. "Joker would be proud of you."

The next day was a day off. My routine had always been 4 days a week training, with Friday, Monday and today, Wednesday, rest days. I came home from work, greeted the dogs, walked Dansa along the promenade, prepared the evening meal, fed them all, and went in to settle down for the evening.

All completely normal.

"Jim, can you come out and look at Fly. She's in her box and coughing," Cherry shouted out to me.

"Be right out, most probably something gone down the wrong way." Fly being a typical Siberian, ate her evening meal as if it would be her last, very, very quickly.

"Alright Fly, what's the matter?" and then I froze.

"Cherry, phone the vets, quick, Fly's got a twisted gut!" I had recognised the symptoms, coughing and bloated stomach, only too well, it was Raider all over again.

I grabbed Fly, put her in the truck and drove like a lunatic to the vets in Bognor Regis, some 6 miles away.

"Hello Mr Bryde, bring her in and let's have a look at her. Possible twisted gut you say."

"Yes, I recognise the symptoms."

"Ok let's quickly give her an X-ray, and we'll know for sure."

"Sorry Mr Bryde, your diagnosis was right. Do you want us to operate or put her to sleep?"

This floored me for a moment, but it was the standard question vets asked with this affliction.

"You have caught her in time, so we can operate, but she has only a fifty-fifty chance of pulling through. Even then, as you are no doubt aware, we can't guarantee she will not get it again. It's also very expensive, and at her age..."

I cut her off at this point.

"Look, money doesn't come into it. She's a very fit girl and I want you to operate, OK?"

"We'll do our best."

Friday evening, after work I made the return journey to Bognor to get Fly.

"Operation has been successful, she's on painkillers so will be a little drowsy. Let her get some rest, and we'll see her again next week."

To me, Fly did not look fine. "Look I know it's a big op, but she doesn't seem right to me."

"It's just the painkillers, she'll be fine."

With that, I took Fly home, still not convinced, but unable to do anything else. After all, they were the Professionals, weren't they?

Fly spent the night in the dog truck, the only place she would settle.

"I don't like this Cherry. Something's wrong."

"We'll see what's she's like in the morning. If she still worries you, take her back."

And that night I didn't sleep at all. Once you are close to your animals you know when something is not right, no matter what you are told.

"Cherry, I'm going downstairs, I can hear Fly crying."

Getting to the truck in double quick time, I let her out, and for a moment I relaxed, she wanted the toilet.

"Good girl Fly. Good girl." But she wasn't. No matter how I tried she would not open her mouth to let me give her a painkilling tablet.

Phoning the emergency number for the vets, this being Saturday morning at 7am, I was connected to an answer phone. An answer phone on an emergency line. I couldn't believe it.

"Cherry I'm taking Fly to the vets in Chichester, she's definitely not well."

Arriving there I had to wait till it opened, and was then told that the vet would see me at 10am, in 2 hours.

"My bloody dog is dying, I want to see the vet," I rather rudely shouted at the receptionist.

"Mr Bryde," the vet said overhearing me, "I have appointments till then. I can't just rearrange my diary for you. Come back at 10 am."

Well to say I exploded with rage would be an understatement.

"You will bloody well see her now. She had a major operation on Wednesday night, and this is an emergency, do your bloody job!"

Needless to say she saw Fly and then panicked.

"You have a very sick dog there, can you take her to Bognor. She might need a further operation."

To save the gory details, I took her to Bognor and to take my mind off it all, I took the dogs out training.

"Jim, Hughie here. You going running tomorrow? I've got some friends coming over and they want to see the dogs run. Can I borrow Fly?" Hughie on the mobile.

"Hughie, didn't want to worry you, but she's in the vets at the moment. She's having a second operation for a twisted gut. Vets have just phoned me and told me she is fine and looking well, and she'll pull through. See you tomorrow."

The time was 2pm.

6pm Saturday 19th June 2010

"Mr Bryde."

"Yes."

"Bognor vets here. I'm afraid that you have received some wrong information. Fly is not responding, she's very weak."

"You phoned only 4 hours ago and said she was fine, and you were very pleased with her."

"I know, I'm terribly sorry. She is really ill."

"She's not going to make it is she?"

"I'm afraid not."

"I don't want her to suffer any more. Let her go."

The phone call to Hughie a couple of hours later was very painful, I think he took the news as hard as me. Fly had died of Peritonitis. I didn't speak to him or indeed anyone else for about a week, I couldn't. I was in a mix of anger and sadness.

I collected Fly on Monday morning, gave the Chief Vet a piece of my mind, the bill was binned, and I never went back there again.

Fly was cremated and her ashes spread on the same trail where I'd spread her Dad's ashes only 25 days earlier.

And as I stood there blubbering remembering the two dogs that had shaped my life, I made a promise to myself.

"Me and Gun will win the next Aviemore for you," and with that I left.

I had made a promise, I would do my best to keep it.

Returning to Selsey I made a beeline to Gun's pen. He had taken his mum's death particularly hard, was off his food and generally down in the dumps.

"Come on Gun, we're going for a walk."

Fifteen minutes later we were back up at Selhurst Park.

Getting Gun out of the truck I was relieved that he seemed a bit like his old self; he gave me a deep growl.

"Come on Gun, say goodbye to your Mum," and I let him sniff the freshly spread ashes.

"That's your mum there Gun; Fly," and his ears pricked up at the familiar name.

"I made a promise to her just before. I said we would go to the next Aviemore and win. No more second places and people telling us we're f.....d. What do you say?"

Gun, rose up, placed his two big paws either side of my head, growled, and then gave me a big kiss.

He'd given me his answer.

Aviemore was on.

Chapter 25

In My Own Time

July and August were very hot and training was limited. My two goals were to get Django's turns and overtaking skills perfected, that was all. Speed would not be a problem, the dogs were perfectly capable of running very fast. So I had all the time in the world to get things right, and that was my intention. But I needed help, so again turned to my training partner of the past twenty years, Hughie. I was convinced that fate was looking down on me and no matter what happened over the next few months, we would win. Totally convinced. But just in case I thought Fate may need a helping hand, we trained, and trained, and trained. Nothing would be left to chance. For the first and only time since I'd started racing I had a balanced team. Gun was in his prime, he could only go downhill from here. Django was so enthusiastic, he would run through a brick wall for me. And Bear and Reef had proved themselves on other teams, winning freely. This was my year, I wouldn't get this chance again, it was MY Time. And I would take it.

I had the added bonus of having three proven leaders, nobody hated anybody else, (believe me, that was a rarity) and I could run any formation I wanted. Luxury, sheer luxury. I was confident.

This new found confidence inspired me in an unusual way.

When Steve had raced in the World Championships in Sweden, the course photographer had taken one of the best pictures of sled dogs I'd ever seen. It showed two dogs in perfect harmony at the start of a race, you'd think the photo had been staged, until you looked closely; the dogs' feet were off the ground. And just out of focus, behind the lead two was another dog. A black dog. That dog was Gun. The lead two... Bear and his litter brother Hobo.

I took the photo and had it professionally enlarged and stuck onto both sides and rear doors of my Transit van. It looked superb blown up, a true "Dog's Bollocks" as the phrase goes. The finishing touch, the Logo, "Leahrno's Siberian Huskies", was plastered on the panels next to the photos. The truck did and still does draw some amazing glances as I drove it around town. I'd made a big statement, now I had to live up to it.

The day after I had it done, my mate Fred came down from Scotland. He was emigrating to France, and would be staying in and around Chichester for the next month.

"Alright Fred, no trouble getting down?"

"No, but I need a new van before I go over. This one's had it. And talking of vans, that's a lovely picture on the side of yours. I've seen it before though, but not like that"

"Yea, I had it enlarged, and cropped. Steve and three other dogs didn't make the final cut."

"You've got a new dog haven't you?"

"Yep, from Gun and Angel."

"What did you call him?"

And I couldn't resist it.

"Sunova."

"Sunova, that's an odd name, where'd that come from?"

"Son of a Gun, get it?" and I laughed "No, his name is Django, come on, let's go give them a run. You've got your Quad with you haven't you?"

Twenty minutes later I had my four hooked up, he had put on his 5; I let the brakes off, and flew. The team had spent all summer stopping and starting, never being allowed to run flat out. Now it was September, and I wanted to see if their speed had suffered. We came in some two minutes ahead of a completely flabbergasted Fred. This was a two time Aviemore winner, and we had just annihilated him.

"Bloody hell, do you always run them so fast?"

"Oh that was a slow run, had the old fella Gun up front, and as you know he's useless," I replied dead pan. Fred had never rated Gun, even though his mother Fly was bred by him.

"Well if you go round Aviemore like that, no one will touch you."

"That's the general idea Fred, but keep it under wraps eh, I don't want the opposition to know."

"Well they won't get it from me, I'll be in France."

The rest of September saw us alternate between running on the rig and Quad. The quad being motorised was fine for speed training, but race days would mean competing on the lightweight race rig, and I needed to find out if they could make the transfer. On 29th September, I decided to break the habit of a lifetime, and time them over a measured 3 mile course. We came in just under 9 minutes, an average 20mph. The Holy Grail for sled dog racers, equivalent to breaking the 4 minute mile. We were in the mix. All we needed to do now was transfer our training times to the real thing... Race day.

And I was so confident of the team's capabilities, that I asked a couple of mates to come down and run them for me, I wanted to see how they would cope under different conditions. And I wished I hadn't. Hughie's grandson Carl, who had raced my dogs since he was 10 years old, now aged 20, came down and beat my time!

Hughie and I followed him on the Quad as he went round the trail without fear, the benefits of youth, and we both winced and screamed as he hit the corners at breakneck speed, never touching the brakes once. We were positive he would tip over, but he didn't, he took the corners like a downhill racer, absolutely awesome. I came away from there glad that he was not an opponent I would face at Aviemore; he didn't own a single dog!

I entered my first race of the season, King's Forest, Thetford due to take place on $30/31^{st}$ October, supremely confident. We'd trained hard, and we were fast, damn fast.

Then 4 days before the race, 26th October, Reef, came into season, and all confidence went out the window. Bear went into a sulk as I put his sister into boarding kennels, and Gun and Django, weren't much better.

But I'd entered so I was going. Angel, my 9 year old spayed bitch, would take her daughter's place. Although they looked like twins, there the similarity ended. Angel could keep up with all my dogs, she just had one glaring fault; she never pulled. Her tug-line was always slack, not piano wire taut as it should be. But she would balance the team.

We raced and came home third, respectable enough. It did however throw my main competitors off the scent. I never mentioned the switch, and to all concerned I'd run my full team. I let them carry on thinking that as I collected my third place trophy and went home to collect Reef and get back on track.

Some hope... Bloody women. Once back home, she steadfastly refused to co-operate, took out her frustrations on her ever suffering brother, and frankly caused chaos. We stopped training for a week.

This was not ideal preparation for the next weekend's racing. We had one training run to get things sorted. That went OK-ish, and we headed off to Suffolk, not totally confident. First day we took it easy, mainly due to being warned at the mushers' meeting that some of the corners, especially the first, would be tricky for fast teams. Well my brakes had a good workout as we came home in second place behind the race favourite Julie Platt. But only by 7 seconds.

The next day, Sunday, we got up at the crack of dawn and headed back down to the race site, having spent an enjoyable night in the Oyster Public House. The drinks flowed and I arrived with a slight hangover, but nothing a few cups of tea wouldn't fix.

Julie took off 2 minutes ahead of me and then we let rip, Django and Gun in lead flying around the now familiar course. We came home a full minute faster than Saturday, and won by 68 seconds overall. Our first victory as a four. And Reef wasn't even at full fitness. We could only get better.

Back at Selhurst Park, the dogs were just getting better and better, and the bonus came when we had a fall of snow. This time round, my iced road did not appear, the council cleared it completely, which I thought was a bloody cheek. I had looked forward to racing on the road again. But as it turned out Hughie, Don, Carl and I had a wonderful week on our own prepared trails, courtesy of a weighted pallet dragged behind the quad. The whole week we never saw a soul, and running three's and four's we had our own winter wonderland.

I had promised another mate Adam, that if he helped me train the dogs I would let him enter a team at the local 1 day rally at Ringwood in The New Forest. He opted to enter the 6 dog, with my four and despite missing the 1st turn, won by a country mile.

The Christmas period was spent upping the mileage to 5 miles four times a week, just getting the team as fit and as fast as I could. So Wednesday 5th January was just another training run. Except I went out later than usual at 7pm, and it was foggy on the Downs. And it was Wednesday. I never trained Wednesdays. But this day I did. And what a training day it turned out to be.

Coming round the corner where I had had the problems turning Dansa in the snow the previous year, we saw the resident herd of Roe deer, run down the track we were headed for. I didn't give it a second thought, nearly every run we saw this herd, and they usually got out of our way, watched us pass, then came back onto the trail to carry on grazing, wild deer indeed!

But we must have split the herd, because as I took the fast right hander, the team and I got the shock of our lives, and we're still alive to tell the tale... luckily. We rounded that corner doing just over 26mph, headlights blaring into the mist from my Quad's headlights. We'd run this course so many times, we could do it blindfolded. Then out of the mist, a young buck jumped... Over the front of the team. Bear was leading with Django, Reef, single swing, Angel and Gun at wheel.

Twenty-six miles an hour, a deer in mid-flight, and Bear leaps up, catches it by the throat and then all hell lets loose. He has the deer on the ground, looking for all the world like the animal he was named after, jaws clamped firmly round its throat. Django, by now has it by an ear. Reef has a rear leg. Me, I'd slammed on the brakes, reversed to stretch out the team and to prevent Angel and Gun getting in on the act. I jumped off and had to react quickly. First I persuaded Reef to let go, which she did quite easily and readily. Pull the lines even tighter so she couldn't re-attach and then onto Django. He had an ear and he was not going to let go so easily. I made as much noise as I could, grabbed him by his considerable ruff, and he let go. Now all that was left was Bear, and he was not going to let go, ever. Even after screaming at him, he held on. The only solution was to pick him up. Even with his immensely powerful jaws and neck muscles, he couldn't hold onto the deer much longer. And neither could I. Something had to give. Bear's jaws opened, he loosened his grip and the deer fell to the ground. It gave a little shriek, struggled to its feet and shot off never to be seen again. A very, very lucky deer. And me, it was only after I had put the dogs back in the truck that I realised how lucky I had been. The roads around this part of the country are littered with the aftermath of deer straying out and being hit by passing cars. The deer usually ends up dead by the side of the road, the offending car, very badly damaged. That damage could have happened to me if I had been a second quicker. Somebody was looking after me after all; Fate!

Chapter 26

Aviemore 2011

Three Wheels on my Wagon

I travelled overnight to Aviemore taking 5 dogs with me, Angel coming along to keep her wimp of a son Django, company. A real mummy's boy if ever there was one. Dansa, now blind and thirteen years old was left behind in Selsey to be looked after by Cherry.

Having only raced sparingly over the past 6 years since I was last here, and having only 1 victory to my name since, I was definitely coming in under the radar – an unknown quantity. I didn't care, I was confident, and that suited me fine.

What didn't suit me were the ground conditions I encountered when I arrived at the race site early Friday morning.

I thought I'd seen some rough trails in my time here, but this was really taking the mickey. Not only was the car park solid ice, so was the trail, the whole four miles. Solid ice.

After I got over the shock of seeing the state of the place, I took Gun out and we went for a slide – and I use the word cautiously – around the trail. It was horrendous, there was no way the event could take place. It would be cancelled, and my dream would be over. Finished.

I persevered however, and after about two miles trekking, up ahead I saw a glimmer of hope. A JCB had never looked so beautiful. It was ripping the ice from the trail.

I found a Forest Ranger who seemed to be in charge, and he told me that by tomorrow morning the whole trail would be cleared, another digger was on its way and they would all be working overnight to make it happen.

It then struck me how far Aviemore had come since those 12 brave souls first ran the event all those years ago. Television crews, including the biggest of the lot; Sky, were here to film the event. The race would take place; money talks.

Seeing the work happening, I relaxed, confident I would be on the start line tomorrow morning. I put Gun away, and made my way up to Aviemore town itself and the "Dalfaber Country Club", to meet up with old friends who would be watching the Weight Pull competition; Aviemore's traditional opening event. This was eagerly anticipated and well supported, mainly by the Alaskan Malamute fraternity, This was what Aviemore meant for them, a proper test of strength for their breed.

If you haven't seen it in real life, it's depicted in "Call of the Wild" Jack London's famous book. In it the half wolf dog "Buck", pulls some amazing weight over a measured distance to win a bet. This is recreated at Dalfaber, the weights on the sled increasing till there is only one dog left standing... The Winner.

Leaving the contest, I wandered back into town and booked into my B and B at the Cairngorm Hotel, where I remained until I went to the "mushers' meeting, 5pm Start at the Coylumbridge Hotel" The draw for the race took place, "number 197 Jim Bryde" was called and I went forward to collect my official race bib. I was drawn near the front of the field, my main competitors, Martin Owen (last year's winner), and Julie Platt, near the end. Satisfied, I left, went and had a traditional "Fish Supper", walked and fed the dogs, had a pint of lager in the bar, and went to bed. Destiny was calling.

6am Saturday morning 22nd January 2011.

My alarm goes off and I awake slowly and wearily get up, a morning person I am not. A quick shower, shave and clean of the teeth and it's downstairs to walk the dogs, anxious for a toilet break after a night in the truck. Into the breakfast bar for a coffee, and I hate coffee, but at this time of the morning that was all that was available, and then the short journey down to the race site.

Despite arriving at the ungodly hour of 6.30am, the place was heaving. I never could understand this fascination in getting there so early. Most of the competition took place from about 10 am onwards, 3 dog started after lunch about 2 pm. Why then the panic to get there so early? But it was the same every year, so I went with the flow. I drove onto the still icy field, parked up and waited.

Ten minutes later, I walked the dogs yet again, watered them, and wandered down to have a look at the official start times that had been put up on a board by the tea wagon.

The area was packed, and as I was leaving I thought I heard something, but wasn't completely sure I had heard correctly.

"Alright Steve (Taylor), how's it going mate?"

"Oh ok Jim, haven't seen you for a while."

"No, but did I just hear correctly, Martin's scratched?"

"Yea, apparently he didn't fancy the trail conditions. You're in the same class aren't you?"

"Yea."

"Well with him out, reckon Julie's got this in the bag"

"You reckon, what about me?"

"Top ten."

"What, I beat Julie by over a minute last time out, still think she'll win?"

"Where was that then?"

"Rendlesham, last November."

"Ok top 5 then."

"Really?"

"Tell you what, Andrea (his wife) is off a couple of minutes ahead of you. If you can beat her you can have her for the night."

"Done" and as I wandered off I wondered if Steve would come to regret his "Mayor of Casterbridge" moment.

With Martin out of the picture, my tactics changed. Flat out speed would no longer be necessary, I needed to make sure of a trouble free run, and get home in a decent time. There was only one dog that could guarantee me that eventuality 100%... Gun.

He'd never taken a wrong turning in his life, not even as a pup in training. Ok he was 8 years old, slowing down a bit, but a rock solid leader. With no idea if the teams in front would be fast or slow, Rookies or experienced, I needed the assurance Gun would give me. He leads. Next to him would be his young son, Django, Reef and Bear at wheel. And so for the first time ever at Aviemore, I relaxed – gone was the usual anxiety, and so were the endless journeys to the tea wagon and toilets. I knew what to expect.

Fifteen minutes to go, my handlers arrived, and one was someone that was totally unexpected.

"Martin, what you doing here?"

"Well I'm not running so I thought I would help out in handling duties" and he gave me a big grin.

"Great, you owe me one anyway."

And as old acquaintances do, we both recalled the last time we raced each other, 6 years ago.

"Always thought Joker was a superb dog, one of the best, and for you and him to lose like you did, well I always thought badly about it. So the least I can do is make sure you get to the start safely, the rest is up to you. But if it's any consolation, hope you win."

"Thanks Martin, I appreciate that. I'll do my best."

And that little passage summed up all that's right in the dog racing community. Of course you want to win, but if you can't you want the best for your opponent, and will gladly help to make it happen; priceless.

"Can you take Django for me, but be careful with him, he's a complete nut."

And I handed him my little live wire of a lead dog. Whereas Gun would just lean into his harness and pull you to the start, Django had not yet mastered the art. His adrenaline at this point was flowing like the proverbial torrent, he twisted and turned and jumped and pulled all the way.

"My god Jim, he's nuts. But he does look like Joker, any relation?"

"Grandson and Great grandson Martin. All the dogs are from him, wouldn't have it any other way."

And as I lined up on that start line, I was back where I started in 1994, running a home bred team. That's where the similarity ended though. These 4 were top quality racing dogs, with the best dog of his generation in their lineage, Jokerman.

"10 seconds to go Jim, Good Luck." Sarah, still doing a sterling job on the mike.

We took off and flew down the trail, me still not observing modern convention by not wearing a helmet. In fact by the standards set by the modern musher, I appeared to be something from an age long gone. No helmet, no shades, no Lycra, no go faster stripes, and no running at the start, a must for the younger fitter generation. Me. I just stood on the footplates, called "Let's go" and the dogs did what they were trained for. Pull me... at speed. The team were doing as I asked, Gun and Django powering up the first hill, catching before we summated the team who had started a minute ahead of us.

"Trail... coming through," as we went past effortlessly.

Down to the horseshoe bend, and I just about managed to slow them enough to round it without coming off. Exiting we took the next left hand bend, moving like the wind. We hit the start of the big downhill section, moving ever so smoothly. On and on we went, perfect harmony from all four, overtaking at will, making the right hand turn at the Loch with ease. I was loving this. Then a sight for sore eyes. A familiar backside up ahead, wearing her number 10 bib, Andrea "Michael Owen" Taylor.

"Trail!" I boomed out, and she looked round, smiled and waved me through. "See you at the finish – have a nice night" and I wondered if Steve had told her of his promise to me.

Gliding past her I couldn't see anyone else ahead, so assumed I had a clear run to the end. I settled down, kept quiet and let the dogs do what they did best; run. I could now relax, enjoy the scenery, finally getting to appreciate the beauty of the Loch, only about 1 mile to the finish.

"What's up Django, problem?" I asked as he kept turning around.

Gun was slowing down, and he had noticed. Now I did as well, and I too became alarmed.

"Come on Gun, nearly home, don't fail me now, hike on."
Nothing.

We were getting slower and slower.

Down to walking pace now, Django was becoming frantic, he wanted to run; his dad didn't.

I was starting to panic, less than 1 mile from the finish and I had a lead dog not wanting to run. Andrea was starting to close us down, was my race over? The dream finished.

I was not going to let this happen. Thinking, I realised that I'd made the classic mistake, taken the first half of the race too fast. Younger dogs and it wouldn't have been a problem. Gun was not a young dog, it was my mistake and I had to think fast and rescue the situation. A slight bend in the trail was nearly upon us, no one would see what I was about to do.

"Easy boys, Easy," as the team slowed to a halt.

Madness, we were taking a break in the most important race of our lives.

"Easy Django, easy," he was going nuts, not at all at ease with this stoppage.

Andrea was closing fast as I started the count.

"5,4,3,2,1, Let's Go."

We took off just as Andrea rounded the bend, less than 30 metres away.

Up the last hill we laboured before finding a second wind and flying across the finish line. We crossed 8 seconds ahead of Andrea, but more importantly, we were in the lead.

Yet in all the panic I still found time to remind Steve, who was waiting for his wife to cross the line,

"Steve, have her round at my place for six, and make sure she's washed and scrubbed up, there's a good lad."

And the place erupted – they had all heard of the "bet".

Without waiting for official confirmation of my time, I drove the team back to my truck, unharnessed, fed and watered them all, and got Angel out. We strolled down casually to the finish to look at the leader board. My name was sitting proudly at the top, 1st. Now this was a big, big surprise after our meltdown, but there it was, Top of the Tree. The time was slow, 16.30 seconds. I'd clocked 14.57 when I lost 6 years earlier. But Julie was still to come in. I prepared myself for looking at a 15 minutes time.

She came over the last hill, visibly tiring and crossed the line to cheers. The crowd had seen the time on the screen.

"Second Jim, Julie's beating you by 25 seconds," Paul Keen, the club President informed me.

"Different story tomorrow Paul, Bear is going up front," and I walked off leaving him open mouthed.

I may have sounded big headed, in truth most people hearing that would come to the same conclusion.

"He's just been soundly beaten and he refuses to lie down, idiot," would be the general consensus.

I knew what had happened out there. Tomorrow was another day. Gun had done what I had asked of him, "get me home within touching distance of the lead". Sunday I would unleash my ace, Mr Bear.

7.30 am Sunday morning 23rd January 2011 I arrived at the car park, walked the dogs, again, and went for a cup of tea. Opposite the wagon was parked a familiar truck, and as I walked over, I saw someone scuttle out of site.

"That Andrea I just seen disappearing?"

"Yes but look, about that promise..."

I saw the rig and the "For Sale" sign.

"Nice rig Steve."

"Yes, it's Andrea's we have two the same and have decided to sell hers."

"That's the Andrea who didn't show last night." I was determined to make him squirm.

"Come on Jim, that was only a joke, I didn't really mean it"

"Yes well, you shouldn't have made the offer, no let up, everyone knows the score, you have to honour it," as I watched him suffer. "Tell you what, knock £50 off the rig and we'll call it quits."

"Done," Steve blurted out, relieved to get out of this without egg on his face.

"No money on me Steve, send you a cheque?"

"Fine, I'll just give it the once over and you can take it away. You going to use it today?"

"Bloody right, mine's getting a bit long in the tooth, one more time round here will most probably sound its death toll."

"You selling him the rig Steve?" Keith Robinson pipes up. He was lying fourth in the race.

"Yep."

"Well make sure you pump up the tyres extra hard, with a bit of luck they'll explode and I'll make up a place and be on the podium." And all said jokingly and in good faith.

"Keith, you'll be lucky to keep 4th place with those donkeys you're running. You should buy the rig yourself, you need all the help you can get."

And the banter carried on back and forth as Steve prepared the rig for racing. Skinny tyres pumped rock hard, adjusted the disc brakes, strapped on a new rig bag, and followed it up with the all-important piece of coloured tape on the handle bars, the sign that the rig had been inspected and fit to race. Steve was after all the official rig inspector for Aviemore.

I had a brand new bit of kit. All I had to do now was work out how to ride it. All rigs are different, and handle differently, much like a new bike. Normally you would try it out on your own training ground, before taking it to a race. I didn't have that luxury; the race was less than two hours away. A couple of goes on the slopes in the car park, minus the dogs, and I was ready.

"Second off number 197, Jim Bryde." Sarah yet again on the Tannoy. "Jim is nearly 30 seconds down on Julie, a lot to make up, but I'm sure he will give it a go. Good luck Jim."

The ten second warning came.

I mounted the rig, it felt good.

The dogs had also heard the warning and slammed into their harnesses, the power even surprising me.

"Hold them wheels tight fellas" I said above the deafening noise "I don't want any false starts," as I crouched down into my favoured starting position, the two snubbers struggling to hold the team back.

5,4,3,2,1,Go.

And if I thought Saturday's start was fast, this was absolutely mental.

The rig practically flew off the line at warp speed.

We made the bottom of the hill, just, and then we really took off. The day before I'd helped the team by scooting up the slope, as everyone does, today I didn't even think about it, Bear and Django were tearing up the old course, and Gun and Reef were matching them stride for stride.

I let them go, this was planned.

I reckoned I needed to catch Julie by the time we hit the Loch turn, about two and a half miles into the race. To carry this out successfully, it would mean going flat out once past the horse shoe bend. If the plan worked, the long slog along the Loch to the finish would ensure she wouldn't have the necessary speed to get away. But to make up a minute by then was a big ask, but we needed to try.

Once we crested the hill, we screamed down towards the only part of the trail that I feared, the dreaded horseshoe bend. I needed to slow the team, we were going too fast, much too fast.

Because rigs are three wheeled, unless you are perfectly balanced going into a corner, you will tip over. Think of the cornering skills of a Reliant Robin, notorious in bends. And I was entering one at warp speed. Time to check out the brakes... I fully locked them. We started skidding, the dogs' power pulling me and the locked rear wheels, easily. But they were slowing down, just, and by the time we entered the bend, with the aid of my right foot dragging on the ground, we crawled through it at walking pace, slow but safe, up a slight hill, take the left hander, then the command the team was waiting for.

"Let's go boys, go get her," and as one Django, Bear, Reef and Gun took off.

When I thought we'd been going fast before, now we were travelling faster than I've ever gone on a rig. The scenery was a blur as I crouched down onto the foot plates, making myself as small as possible, my head just popping over the handlebars to check where we were going.

Down, and down we went, effortlessly, until I saw ahead what I was looking for, a rig in the distance. This had to be Julie, the plan had worked. But it wasn't. It turned out to be a back-marker from the earlier 6 dog race. We passed her and carried on and out of the corner of my eye I saw a team go around the next corner.

I took the corner seconds later, much too fast and was greeted by a wonderful sight... the leader of the race; Julie. She was less than 20 metres ahead. My plan had worked.

"Well done fellas, take a breather, then we'll take her."

BANG!

"What the hell was that?"

My right tyre had exploded and I was now running on two wheels, cursing that bastard Keith, Steve, in fact anyone who came into my head.

I had literally blown it – my race was over. I'd been in this situation before, in 3 dog class, years ago and from being in the lead, came in 2nd. But a ray of light suddenly switched on in my head. Julie was up ahead, dogs being dogs will naturally chase any ahead of them, and Siberians were the world's best at this. As long as I balanced on the left footplate, keeping my weight off my damaged right wheel, we would be ok. The team would chase Julie, they would get a "tow". I just had to make sure she didn't get too far ahead or the "elastic band" effect would snap and she would leave us in her wake.

And I started singing, anything to keep my mind off what could happen: the wheel getting snagged up with the shredded tyre and locking up completely; making it impossible to turn.

"Three wheels on my wagon, and I'm still rolling along,
Those Cherokees are after me, hippty happty, happty li"

That bloody song came into my head and I just couldn't get it out.

"Two wheels on my wagon, and we're still rolling along"

Julie was powering ahead, the elastic band was still holding, the dogs still running.

"One wheel on my wagon, and we're still rolling along"

I hated that song, but it was having the desired effect, it was keeping me occupied, and time was flying.

I was just starting to get into the final verse "No Wheels", when into sight was a sign for sore eyes; "No Row".

We were at the final hill, no more than 800mts to go, we'd made it.

"Don't do anything stupid, just stay behind and you've won. Be sensible," the little voice in my head.

And that would be the sensible and logical thing to do.

Me, I wanted to win, and in style, sensible went out the window.

I was only 30 metres behind Julie, her team were tiring, while mine had been held back and still fresh, so I went for it.

"All the way home boys!" I cried, the signal for the team that the end was in sight and to give it all that they had. The surge came, and I jumped off the rig and ran up the hill, giving them all the help I could.

We caught Julie at the top, I was about to call trail, but realised that she wouldn't pull over and let us pass. This was the No Right of way area, every one for themselves.

We were both back on our rigs now and over the small bridge, racing side by side, and took the left hand bend to enter the final 250 metres straight, the finish line in sight.

My plan was to take Julie on this bend, and steam ahead and take the tape first. I manoeuvred into position on the rig, and immediately realised I had made a mistake. In my eagerness to win, I had forgotten my knackered wheel, there was no grip at all on the right hand side of the rig. And it was still icy. Whilst Julie took it perfectly, I slid into the pine trees along the trail, and had to hang on for dear life as the rig tipped. I slammed on the brakes, adjusted my weight and got all three wheels back on the ground.

"You idiot Bryde, You Total idiot," there was that voice again.

Julie was by now about 50 metres ahead, and had crossed the line to huge cheers.

"Come on Gun, let's do this for Fly, all the way home," and we crossed 3 seconds later, but more importantly, 28 seconds ahead overall.

We had achieved what we had set out to do.

Not second.

We Had Won.

Aviemore 2011 C class Winner. J T Bryde. Team Leahrno.

Chapter 27

It's Just Another Day

Sunday Morning January 26, 2014, France

I, Cherry, the dogs and China the Bengal cat, now live in France. After winning Aviemore, I had achieved my goal, and we thought it was time to retire to our own "place in the sun". Between us, Gun and I had placed second 9 times at Aviemore, and now we were both winners. No longer second best. No longer washed up. We had earned our time in the sun, job done.

But before leaving though I had received a phone call.

"Hi you don't know me, but I'm a mate of Fred's. I'm after a couple of Siberian bitch puppies. Are you planning to breed soon?"

"No intentions at the moment, but I'll give you a call if I change my mind."

Two months later.

"Hi mate, listen I'm planning to mate Reef to Django, my two lead dogs. Still want two girls?"

"Certainly do."

That phone call put into motion the reason I was now sitting by my mobile, in rural France, waiting for a text.

Having checked the guy out, I went up to see his kennels, and more importantly, to see if he could handle a fast race team, my Aviemore 4. He passed both tests with flying colours. I also knew 2 girls would not be enough. Not after running my team. He would take however many pups Reef had, he just didn't know it yet.

November 4th 2012

I phoned him again.

"Hi mate," I said. "You ever see Jaws?"

"Yea of course, why do you ask?"

"Do you remember the part where Richard Dreyfus first sees the shark, and what he says?"

"Course I do, we're gonna need a bigger boat. But enough of this daft Quiz, has she had them yet?"

"You sitting down?"

"Why?"

"You're gonna need bigger kennels, number 7 has just been born."

Sharp intake of breath.

"I'll take the lot."

February 5th, 2013 I delivered to Snowdonia, 7 puppies. Four boys, Quarrie, Gravil, Granite and Boulder. Three girls, Cheffois, Cholet, and Chantonnay.

And now at just 14 months old, and still babies, they had been entered in B class Aviemore, Six dog 2014.

The text buzzer sounded.

"Turns out we broke course record yesterday. Horrendous conditions today, worst ever, but won by 10 seconds to win overall by 36 seconds. We did it!"

The guy?

Gareth, the prodigy, who we beat in 3 dog, Pembury.

My Aviemore Dreams had not only come true, they had reached another level.

I had bred the fastest team in Britain.

The Fastest.

The Best.

Dreams do come true.

I turned to the dog sitting at my feet.

"Can you read that Gun, the grandkids won," and he stands up, puts his paws either side of me and growls.